*Flexible
Working Hours
in Practice*

Flexible Working Hours in Practice

Michael Wade

Gower Press

First published in Great Britain by Gower Press Ltd, Epping, Essex, CM16 4BU

© *M. Wade and Gower Press 1973*

ISBN 0 7161 0197 1

Filmset and printed by Thomson Litho, East Kilbride, Scotland

Contents

1 Origins of flexible working hours   9
Messerschmitt–Bölkow–Blohm   11
Time clocks   12
Overtime   14
Employee attitudes   14
Benefits to management   16

2 Varieties of flexible working time   19
White-collar status problems   20
Effect on absenteeism   22
Initial British experience   23

3 Installing flexible working time: J. Walter Thompson
GmbH   25
Working with the *Betriebsrat*   26
Initial memorandum to employees   27
Management version of the rules   28
The modification that was accepted   29

4 Time-recording systems   33
Manual systems   33
Mechanical recording: Lufthansa   34
Mechanical recording: Hengstler system   38

5   *Flexible working time installed by management :*
    Wiggins Teape Ltd   43
    Introducing the scheme   44
    Installing the complete scheme   51
    Unjustified suspicions   51
6   *Flexible working time installed by joint committee :*
    Pilkington Brothers Ltd   55
    Pilot scheme   56
    Time recording   57
    Instructions to staff   57
    Results of the trial   61
7   *Effects of flexible working*   67
    Advantages to employees   67
    Some disadvantages to employees   69
    Advantages to management   70
    Disadvantages to management   73
    TUC's view of limitations   74
8   *Four-day, forty-hour week*   79
    Four-day working in Britain   80
    Canadian experience   82
    Australian experience   84
    Worker and management attitudes in Britain   84
    Fatigue   85
    Future developments   86
9   *A system based on trust : Schreiber Wood*
    Industries Ltd   89
    Shopfloor starting-point of system   90
    Role of shopfloor committee   92
10 *Probable developments*   97
Appendix 1   Planning and implementation checklist   103
Appendix 2   50 leading organisations using flexible
    working hours   107
Index   109

Illustrations

1:1   Meaning of flexible working hours   10

4:1   Lufthansa clock card   36

4:2   Hengstler time-recording equipment   40

5:1   Document issued by Wiggins Teape to employees participating in a trial of flexible working time   45

5:2   Attitude survey by Wiggins Teape   49

5:3   Example of a Wiggins Teape diary sheet   50

5:4   Extract from Wiggins Teape manual for flexible working   52

6:1   Pilkington Brothers survey: average time of arrival   62

6:2   Pilkington Brothers survey: average time of departure   63

6:3   Pilkington Brothers survey: length of lunch interval   64

9:1   Schreiber Group: weekly absenteeism/lateness record   93

9:2   Schreiber Group: personal absence record   94

10:1   London & Manchester Assurance: employee's personal record of hours worked   99

Acknowledgement

To Jim Dening, Development Director of Gower Press, who provided the implementation checklist in Appendix 1.

1

Origins of flexible working hours

This book describes a number of organisations in the UK and Europe in which there is a belief that hours of work should not be fixed. They put this belief into practice in various ways, the most popular of which is usually called 'flexible working time' or 'flextime'.

Basically the working day is divided into two parts: a 'core time' around midday and 'flexible periods' during the morning and afternoon.

Employees can vary, on an individual basis, the times at which they start and finish work. They do not have to start 'on time' and can vary their times from day to day. However, they must be present during the core time, say between 10 00 and 16 30, except for lunch breaks. They can, therefore, start at any time between, say, 08 30 and 10 00 and stop between 16 30 and 18 30, so long as they work at least the contracted number of hours per day, week or month (see Figure 1:1).

Obviously these times vary between industry, area and country; the basic model can be easily modified to suit all customs, individual needs and commuting conditions. In some schemes only the length of the working week or month

Figure 1 :1   Meaning of flexible work hours

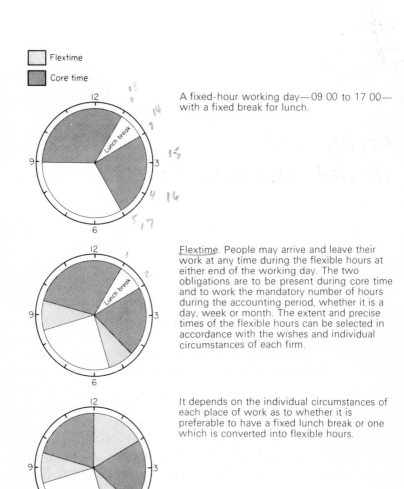

A fixed-hour working day—09 00 to 17 00—with a fixed break for lunch.

Flextime. People may arrive and leave their work at any time during the flexible hours at either end of the working day. The two obligations are to be present during core time and to work the mandatory number of hours during the accounting period, whether it is a day, week or month. The extent and precise times of the flexible hours can be selected in accordance with the wishes and individual circumstances of each firm.

It depends on the individual circumstances of each place of work as to whether it is preferable to have a fixed lunch break or one which is converted into flexible hours.

is fixed; if a worker starts early and finishes late one day, he can take time off the next day, or in the next week, or month, in some systems.

Messerschmitt–Bölkow–Blohm

The idea of flexible working time was conceived by the personnel manager of the German aerospace company Messerschmitt–Bölkow–Blohm GmbH. The system was introduced in 1967 at the company's headquarters at Ottobrunn on the outskirts of Munich, which then had 3,000 white-collar employees in administration and R & D.

Public transport to the MBB offices was inadequate and only one-quarter of the workers used the company's subsidised bus. The majority had their own cars.

This resulted in a very bad traffic congestion problem. Each day there was a long queue at the main gate and at the clocking-in points. Each day employees eased off work some 15 minutes early so that they could head the queue to clock out. Productivity suffered and so did morale.

The cause of this waste was the fixed working hours. Starting time was 07 20, finishing 17 00 (Friday 16 30) with a 30-minute lunch break. (The early start is typical of German white-collar employment.)

Other firms had solved this problem by staggering the times at which various departments started and finished work. MBB considered this but were also interested in the experiments in 'variable' working time being carried out in German firms then. In the variable system, an employee has complete freedom to choose when he works. But he must complete a set number of contracted hours and ensure that a 'deputy' is available to carry out any essential work that could occur during his absence. This system was welcomed by creative workers—in design, research and publicity, for example—because of the freedom they were given to work at their own pace (which was often faster than the fixed-time company pace).

Herr Hillert, MBB's personnel manager, was impressed by the personal freedom that variable working gave but felt that it could be applied to only a limited group of workers. His solution was a compromise between variable and staggered hours which came to be known as *Gleitzeit* ('gliding' or 'sliding' time) in German and 'flextime' or 'flexible working time' (FWT) in English.

In MBB's flexible-time system, employees can arrive when they like between 07 00 and 08 00, and leave at any time between 16 00 and 18 00. They must, however, be present during the core time, which is 08 00 to 16 00 (15 30 on Fridays), except for a fixed 48-minute lunch break. They must also work their total monthly contractual hours, plus or minus 10 hours, the balances being carried forward into the next month.

Arrival and departure times are recorded on punched cards in time clocks placed near offices. Every 10 days these are fed into a computer, giving a total of the number of hours worked. If an employee works anything up to 10 hours more than the norm in any month he is not paid for this 'credit balance' as overtime, but instead is entitled to an equivalent amount of free time in the following month. If he has a debit balance, he can make this up during the flexible periods at a later date.

Each employee's time 'credits' or 'debits' are stamped on his monthly pay slip, and he has a continually updated record of the number of hours he has worked.

Time clocks

There is an ingrained prejudice against clocking in and out among both white-collar and manual workers. In Germany, there is a legal requirement that if a system of time recording operates, everyone from directors down must abide by the rules of the system.

It is generally true that in the UK clocking is applied to

manual employees and not to white-collar employees. UK companies that have been involved in single-status experiments (giving works and staff employees similar conditions) have often started with the abolition of clocking.

Initially, there were fears in MBB that the Ottobrunn scientists and engineers would find the clocking system a little undignified. But there was a need for time records in case of disputes and so that employees could have an up-to-date record of the hours they had worked. Manual recording and individual time meters were rejected as being unreliable or too costly, and so were punched-card/magnetic-tape systems because of their lack of visual control.

The time clocks chosen, which take a standard 80-column punched card, pre-punched with each employee's name and number, enable project costing to be controlled efficiently. Each serves between 70 and 120 employees and are controlled by a central master clock. They are set to record in tenths of an hour, to simplify calculations. These are helped by a ready-reckoner which compares arrival and departure times to give total hours worked each day. Lunch breaks are fixed (and staggered by department) and so are not clocked.

The working month is divided into three 10-day periods: from the 1st to the 10th the 11th to the 20th, and the 21st to the month end. The contracted 'standard' number of total hours to be worked in any period are posted with each time clock. They are 8.9 hours a day Monday to Thursday, and 8.4 hours on Friday. Each employee clocks in and out each day, and then writes in a calculated total of hours worked. At the end of each period he completes the card (so he knows the time debit or credit situation) and this is checked for accuracy at his time clock's control point. The card is then signed, stamped, countersigned by the department head, and sent to the punch room.

When cards have been punched, fed into the computer and checked for any errors, 10-day summaries are produced showing hours worked and credit/debit balances taken into account. At the month end a composite time record is assembled which lists every employee, be he fully employed, shift or staff worker. Any time debit exceeding the permitted limit of 10 hours per month is investigated at this stage, and overtime work and payments are also examined.

Overtime

Overtime still exists in a flextime scheme. Work outside 'normal finishing' hours is counted as overtime only if an employee is requested to continue with a job at the request of his superior. These hours are recorded on a special form by the department head. An employee can then either be paid for them at agreed rates for the time when the work took place (on a weekend, bank holiday etc.) or he can take time off in lieu, which is scaled up by the percentage used to work out the overtime rate. To prevent overtime 'credits' building up over too long a period, all outstanding ones are paid in cash at the end of every December. In any case time records are only kept by the department for six months at a time.

Employee attitudes

The flextime system is obviously an extremely fair way of adding up hours actually worked and so the feared objections to 'undignified clocking in' have never materialised. Instead, any residual prejudice to a soulless punctuality check has been converted to a highly favourable view of the costing system. In an opinion poll run by the MBB personnel department in 1969, not one employee expressed any resentment. Instead the majority claimed that the time clock, far from being a symbol of oppression, stands for much greater personal freedom.

The reaction of all employees to other questions in the survey echo this belief. Some 65 per cent felt that working conditions were much better as a result of flexible working hours—and this percentage was about the same for salaried staff, married, and single employees. Only 1.1 per cent felt that conditions were worse, and 'don't knows' averaged 6.2 per cent.

The advantages of the system to the employees were seen by them as: better balance between work and private life (30.6%), easier travel (23.5%), better fit between work rhythm and work load (21.3%), more freedom (12.3%), avoidance of morning rush (6.6%) and better fit of work to individual performance (5.7%).

Only seven employees reported unspecified 'personal disadvantages' and some 79 saw a disadvantage in the reduced time available for communication. This last point is quite important. It is often feared that flexible work hours mean that employees will probably often be missing when they are most needed. However, many companies actually welcome the fact that telephoning tends to happen only during core time (because that is when the person one is trying to reach will certainly be at his desk). The practical effect is that the flexible hours are quiet periods during which individuals can work undisturbed.

In MBB, the vast majority of employees are happy with the system. In his book *Flexible Working Hours*, which thoroughly details the MBB experience, J. Harvey Bolton, an Urwick Orr consultant, says:

> People are now responsible for their own work and for the rhythm of their work. There is no longer any sitting around watching the clock for the time to go home. When, in order to get his work done, an employee works longer, he knows that the time will be taken into account. If he needs a day off, he can take half a day's holiday allocation and add the other half day under the flexible working hours arrangement, either from time in hand, or as time he will make up later.
>
> On two occasions it proved possible to keep the offices closed for days which fell between a weekend and a holi-

day; by arrangement between management and staff, employees enjoyed a four-day holiday and the firm lost nothing. This has now become standard practice and meets with general approval.

Benefits to management

From the company's point of view, the benefits have been very real and initial fears have proved groundless. Bolton says of MBB:

> In the early stages, management had doubts as to what would happen when employees were allowed to be in debit of up to 10 hours each. These fears were misplaced. Since the scheme started, the employees— as a body—have never been in debit; on the contrary, they have a fairly constant credit equivalent to 3 hours 50 minutes per man. Only 1 per cent of employees exceed the permissible 10 hours minus, and in eight out of every ten cases this is found to be due to some missing entries on the card. Only in two cases out of a thousand is the cause illness in the family or some other emergency; almost invariably such debts are liquidated in the second month following.
>
> The thought that the cut-off point of plus hours (only 10 of which may be carried forward) creates an *additional* profit for the company is probably unrealistic; it is likely that these additional hours were strays worked, but remained unrecorded in the post.

Nevertheless, the company has profited considerably by the scheme. It has estimated for a start that it saves some £16,000 per month in increased productivity and lower absenteeism. As Bolton says:

> Employees arrive fresh, their morale high. Getting the job done is now more important than timekeeping. An

employee will finish a job, or continue it to a natural break rather than interrupt it and have to rethink it the following morning; this reduces unnecessary recapitulation, and increases efficiency. At peak periods the arrangement is much preferred to doing overtime one week and hanging around the next because there is not enough work available. There is less dishonesty, fewer fairytales are told in order to get time off, and there is definitely less malingering.

2

Varieties of
flexible working time

By late 1971, before any British company experimented with flexible working time, some 2,000 European companies, employing about 1 million workers, the majority of them white-collar staff, were operating flexible working systems. In most cases, it seems, pressure from the workforce has been mainly responsible for the introduction of flexible working hours, with management becoming more and more in favour as benefits have accrued.

With this large number of users, many varieties of the flexible working hours concept have been put into practice and many different problems have been solved.

The simplest type of flexible scheme is that adopted by J. Walter Thompson GmbH and described in Chapter 3. A fixed number of hours must be put in each day and employees must attend during the core time but the day can start early or late to taste. For example, the core time could cover a six-hour period, with a fixed lunch break. This would allow staff the flexibility of arriving and leaving within two hours on either side of the core time, and there would be no carry forward of credit or debit time.

Greater flexibility can be obtained if the core time is split into two periods (for example, 09 00–12 00 and 14 00–17 00) with three, flexible, two-hour bands in which to make up the contractual eight hours and take lunch (07 00–09 00, 12 00–14 00, and 17 00–19 00). A few German companies have applied this system successfully since 1969. It is useful where staff traditionally return home for lunch, and it allows an employee to start later, yet finish earlier than another, if he so wishes.

The more extended system that covers a flexible working day has also been tried out in some German companies and by Wiggins Teape (Chapter 5) and Pilkington Brothers (Chapter 6) in the UK. Here staff may carry forward credit or debit hours from day to day within a month. They are allowed a greater degree of responsibility, to cope with the fluctuations in their work load without having to work overtime, and need only attend during the daily core times, completing their contractual hours at their convenience. At the end of the month some debit or credit hours may be carried forward to the next month.

White-collar status problems

Obviously there are some categories of staff—like canteen workers, chauffeurs, commissionaires, and telephonists—to whom flexible working hours cannot always be applied. In this respect, it might seem that the system could create friction between white- and blue-collar workers, by increasing 'status differentials'. One company, however, has used it to eliminate those very grievances—Sandoz AG, the Swiss chemical and pharmaceutical manufacturer.

Its application of flexible hours has some special features: a two-part core time, no clocking-in, and an extension (in a modified form) to maintenance, production and transport employees.

Introduced in April 1970, then covering some 2,000 white-collar workers in Basle, the system is based on a working day of eight hours 35 minutes. Core time runs from 09 00 to 12 00, and 14 00 to 16 00; flexible periods are 07 00–09 00, 12 00–14 00 and 16 00–19 00. A 45-minute lunch break is compulsory and the maximum credit or debit time allowance is 10 hours per month.

Now obviously production workers had to be excluded from working these flexible hours, when the system was extended to cover some 6,500 factory workers. Production personnel work shifts, but they are free to choose a starting time between 06 00 and 08 00 (shifts beginning at 07 00, 07 40 and 08 00). But once they have joined a shift, they must remain with it for a month, after which, with a supervisor's approval, they can vary their schedule.

This system has undoubtedly created a much greater sense of individual equality. The discrepancy between office and factory staff has been further eroded by paying all employees on a monthly basis. Further, office workers who once worked a 42½-hour week instead of the 43-hours put in by production now work five minutes more each day to even things out.

The 'honour' system of timekeeping has been another great leveller. The time clock was abolished by Sandoz AG in June 1970. Since then each employee has been responsible for correctly completing his time recording sheet, which is inspected by his immediate superior, and is accountable for the time spent.

The introduction of these techniques certainly caused friction, at first, in the company's middle management. Some managers chafed at the idea that they could no longer compel subordinates and secretaries to get in early, or stay late, as they wished, but the system has had an important disciplinary impact on executives. They have had to organise their time more carefully, and in the process some of them have lost a few illusions about how hard they work. For example, late hours at the office have often been dictated by long breaks earlier in the day.

This need for stricter self-discipline, to allow subordinates greater freedom and flexibility, may also have been behind the initial objection of supervisors and foremen when the scheme was 'extended' to the factory. There has also been resistance to greater informalities encouraged by the company such as acceptance of a 'leisure' style of dress as opposed to formal business suits.

Obviously, the effect of flexible working time on Sandoz executives has been profound. The results to the company are simply expressed. Switzerland has an acute labour shortage. The national average labour turnover is 25 per cent each year. Sandoz's turnover was 14.6 per cent in 1970 and 12.4 per cent in 1971.

Effect on absenteeism

Absenteeism has been considerably reduced by flexible working schemes. This has been particularly proved in France, where interest in flex time is intense and a great public debate has centred around the theme of de Chalendar's book *L'Aménagement du Temps*.

One French company, Bergerat Monnoyeur, in a recent pilot scheme in its accounts and data processing department showed a dramatic cut in absenteeism of around 75 per cent. Some 25 employees, mostly women, were involved—the entire department, including the manager, clocking in and out each time they left.

The scheme has a core time from 09 15 to 16 30 and flexible periods of 08 00 to 09 15 and 16 30 to 19 00. It has a 45-minute 'compulsory' lunch break starting at 12 30. Employees can, if they want to, take an extra 30 minutes over lunch, which can be 'worked off' in a flexible period.

Morale in the department was rated as very high some 25 days after the inception of the scheme. Employees also were more cooperative—in one case working voluntarily 10 hours in one day to clear a bottleneck of work. The department head also praised the increased sense of individual responsibility shown. In a recent interview, he cited the case of an impromptu party which had occurred in the office one evening. When it started, at 17 00, 23 out of the 25 employees spontaneously 'clocked out', as if they had left the office.

Initial British experience

Nearly 150 British companies were operating pilot schemes at the time this book went to press. About 20,000 employees are involved.

Nearly all the trial schemes have been introduced in departments that contain monthly paid, white-collar staff, who normally work very little overtime. There have been several early surveys of effectiveness but most managements seem to feel that a one-year trial period is necessary for real evaluation, to take sales peaks, holidays etc. into proper account.

About 60 per cent of these British schemes use specially developed time-recording equipment. Most of the others use existing, modified, time clocks and a few are trying out the 'honour' system, with employees completing their own time-sheets.

The flexibility of the schemes is as varied. The flexible periods before core time vary from 15 minutes to three hours. The carry forward of credit and debit times is also different in many cases (a minority being as much as 10 hours) and the amount and degree of supervision also varies, depending inversely on whether 'honour', converted, or 'precision' time-recording equipment is used.

Two factors are standard in all cases: the accounting period—one month—and the care taken by all managements to detail all the advantages and disadvantages of the system in joint consultation before introducing flexible hours.

This full consultation is thought to be extremely important.

All companies recognised that there were several categories of staff that could not be given flexible working hours without straining the system. All companies took the trouble to detail the difficulties involved to the employee concerned, and in some cases have introduced staggered hours to cover the longer working day. These measures, and their acceptance, have had a positive effect on the establishment of all schemes.

Of course, as with any new system, problems have occurred. Difficulties have arisen with the 'credit' times allocated to employees who travelled a lot on business. The standard working day with no other credit involved that was applied to these cases obviously fostered grievances.

Both management and employees have experienced noticeable benefits in all but one of these schemes. Several companies feel that the system helps to plan work (highlighting individuals with too heavy work loads) and the reappraisal of time-keeping attitudes was beneficial.

Almost all employees are enthusiastic to such a degree that they express unwillingness to return to their original routineness. As a majority of the companies concerned are planning to extend their schemes in the near future, it seems that the initial British experiment with German *Gleitzeit* has been a success.

3

Installing
flexible working time :
J. Walter Thompson GmbH

The British experience, as well as that of companies all over
Europe, shows that the successful introduction of flexible
working time depends directly on the careful initial discussions between management and staff representatives.

All British companies stress the need to prepare employees
and management fully for the changes that flexible working
will introduce. Trade-union representatives must also be kept
fully informed from the outset.

At Allen and Hanburys Ltd, a member of the Glaxo
Group, which introduced a pilot scheme covering 1,300
employees at Ware, Hertfordshire, in January 1972, the
Transport and General Workers' Union was involved in the
negotiations. Initial discussions were held with the union and
separate meetings followed with the employees concerned,
with the union representative present. In the weeks before the
scheme was introduced employees in the department were
given the opportunity of discussing the scheme with management, either individually or in small groups.

The first stage for a company, *before* meetings between management and staff, is for management to be quite clear about which type of flexible work arrangement it wants to install. Work-load fluctuations and communication patterns must be established, and the basic types of flexibility thoroughly understood. Management must clarify the advantages and disadvantages of flexible hours and decide the approximate viable core time, flexible periods and credit/debit carry-forward hours. Finally, and most important, it must decide its policy regarding overtime (and its compensations) and the method of time recording.

These last two factors proved to be real bones of contention with J. Walter Thompson's Frankfurt subsidiary, despite the most careful initial handling.

Working with the Betriebsrat

From the start, the management of J. Walter Thompson GmbH worked closely with its *Betriebsrat* or works council. This council is a legally constituted body of staff representatives, which exists in every German firm. Trade-union allegiance is not a condition of membership of the committee.

The numbers of *Betriebsrat* members depend on the total number of company employees. The one in J. Walter Thompson GmbH has nine members and there are elections to it every four years by secret ballot. The *Betriebsrat* members elect their own leaders. The leader at JWT comes from the television department and has been with JWT for 20 years. His deputy is a young copywriter. The others include an account planner, a cleaning woman and a book-keeper. They meet monthly or more often if they wish. The committees have substantial powers. For example, if a firm wants to fire a man and its *Betriebsrat* objects, the matter goes before the court.

At JWT the *Betriebsrat* wanted to shorten the working week from 40 hours to 37½ hours. Management wanted better attendance and thought of *Gleitzeit* with 40-hour attendance as a compromise.

Once agreement between management and *Betriebsrat* had been reached, the next phase was to test the idea of the system with the rest of the staff. The main dilemma was that while the creative employees within the agency would be sympathetic to flexibility (ideas never come on a set schedule) they would be unlikely to accept the discipline of a time-recording system.

Initial memorandum to employees

So the *Betriebsrat* called for a vote on the principle of the scheme. It sent a detailed memorandum to all staff. This started: 'The "social package deal" that has been discussed over the past few months between the management and your representatives concerns conditions of work, shorter hours, general staff policies and "flexible working hours". We are now in a position to discuss this last point with you. We have looked at examples introduced in other companies and are convinced that flexible working hours offer important advantages to you.'

It then outlined a basic scheme, which allowed employees who did not wish to participate to continue working their fixed times within the system. Then came the most important question, concerning the time-recording equipment.

It was headed 'Do you want the little box?' showed the diagram of a 'precision' time clock, and read:

> Without this small piece of equipment the advantages of flexible working hours cannot be enjoyed. The little box is a 'thinking' piece of electronic equipment which is linked to the computer. When you enter or leave the building and press the correct button, your working-time and free-time 'accounts' will be reported on a punched card. It is all very discreet. No contact is necessary with

your boss, the computer department, or any other controller.

The 'little box' is quite different from the ordinary time clock—it is silent and there is no record to show whether you were early or late.

No one in the company would be excluded from using the 'little box'; not even top management. It would provide us with the freedom to manoeuvre with working time and time off. It would give management the chance they are looking for, to recognise the hours employees put into their jobs.'

The memorandum asked for a vote on the ideas of flexible working hours and 'attitudes' to the time clock and was sent out in May 1970. Two weeks later the voting was reported: 92.1 per cent favoured *Gleitzeit*, 6 per cent were against.

Management version of the rules

The rules of the system were then drawn up and, on 8 September 1970, the management prepared a document for all employees. This set out the basics of the scheme and envisaged implementation from 1 October 1970. An employee could start work at any time between 07 30 and 09 30, and finish between 16 30 and 18 30. A one-hour lunch break could be taken some time between 12 30 and 14 00. Core times (which JWT called 'key periods'—possibly a better descriptive term) were 09 30 to 12 30 and 14 00 to 16 30.

Having covered the scheme's outlines, this document then went on to say that any overtime which had to be performed should be compensated for in the form of time off, taken within one calendar month. No more than two periods per month, of four successive working hours each (equalling a half-day, either in the morning or afternoon), would be granted for this. Any other time to be made up for would be taken during the flexible period (at the most, two working hours per day) and a 'credit' account of up to 10 hours of uncompensated overtime could be transferred to the next month. Similarly a 10-hour debit period was the maximum allowed.

The document next described the envisaged time-recording arrangement: 'The time-taker ("little box") and the time sheets enable the employee himself, the manager of the department, and the board to check the number of working hours performed. The time-takers are placed at the entrances to the individual departments or floors. Every member receives a "time card". With this, he registers when he starts and when he finishes work, the beginning and end of his lunch hour, and any interruptions to his work due to official and non-official reasons, by pressing the relevant buttons on the time-taker, which check his coming and going.'

It ended with a description of time computation. However, this well-planned communication was never sent out. Instead of the company starting the scheme on 1 October 1970, it was not until 1 February 1971, that an extremely modified version of *Gleitzeit* finally appeared.

Maybe the difference in emphasis detailing the time-recording equipment between the *Betriebsrat's* memorandum and the management's document of rules reveals the gulf in thinking. At any rate, the company dropped the idea of using any form of little box. Carl-Albrecht von Treuenfels of the company's personnel department reports: 'There were quite a few people who did not like the idea of being checked by a computer. So the order for a five-year lease of the equipment was cancelled.' The cancellation fee was about £2,300.

The modification that was accepted

The company then went ahead with a modified version of the scheme, showing (together with its *Betriebsrat*) firmness and clear thinking in a very difficult situation. Its memorandum of 28 January 1971 is self-explanatory.

The catchword 'flexible hours' has prompted all sorts of actions and reactions in our house over the past few months. Waves of discussion have swept the company. Advocates, sceptics and opponents juggled with the new idea. The start had to be postponed. A committee consisting of members of management, the *Betriebsrat* and various employees have sat down together and finally came up with a solution.

As a result, management have decided to introduce new working-hour regulations starting next Monday, 1 February 1971. These new rules have the chief advantage that our employees can from now on keep their hours flexible because they can start their work at individual times most convenient to them and finish work in the afternoon correspondingly.

Each employee may begin his daily work any time between 7 30 and 9 30, provided this does not interfere with internal departmental decisions or schedules. Each working day will thus invariably end 9 hours after the start of work (8 hours working time, 1 hour for the lunch break). For example, a staff member arriving at the office at 08 50 cannot leave before 17 50.

Attendance books will no longer be kept in the reception area. Instead, we have decided to introduce a practice already adopted by other agencies. Each department will carry an attendance list on which each member will from now on enter and sign the time of arrival in the morning and the leaving time in the afternoon. The lists will be countersigned by the respective head of department to be sent on the next day to the Personnel Department where they will be kept for a certain time, in compliance with professional unions' and insurance companies' stipulations.

Today or tomorrow the respective department heads, who will be held responsible for the working hours being kept, will discuss the matter with you. To make sure that each staff member has been duly informed about these changes he will sign a declaration to that effect which he will receive from his department head.

Both management and the *Betriebsrat* sincerely hope that JWT has thus moved an important step closer toward more liberal working conditions and regulations, even if no hours can be compensated for over days and weeks for the time being. Our experience during the next few months to come will then show what kind of alterations can or should be made.

The experience, subsequently, has been a fairly happy one. The JWT personnel department's view is that working conditions have certainly improved. People are generally happy to come in later. As for the 'quiet time' periods, only those that arrive at 07 30 really benefit. Above all, the system is attractive to staff—to such a degree that it is mentioned in recruitment advertisements, and many secretaries now request it.

There has been no measurable increase in office costs since flexible working hours were introduced. Some people had to change their working time and their shifts (the telephone exchange, for example). Furthermore a receptionist had to be hired for three hours in the evening.

The JWT system then is popular and will probably develop in the next two to three years. Certainly by carrying time forward from month to month, and it is possible that attitudes to clocking in will change, although staff now have to write down the times they start and leave anyway.

4

Time-recording systems

The experience of J. Walter Thompson GmbH shows clearly that, although some system of recording is vital to the success of flexible working hours, an ill-judged system of time recording can completely alienate staff.

Manual systems

The staff at the Ministry of Transport in Bonn have applied the easiest, cheapest form of time recording using a clearly printed manually completed card. This was divided into four one-week columns, each subdivided into the working days of the week. Columns for starting and finishing times, daily hours worked and weekly totals completed the card.

An even simpler card has been used for manual recording in Britain by Pakcel Converters Ltd. This main printing subsidiary of British Sidac Ltd introduced a permanent flexible working scheme for its St Helens administrative staff in January 1972, after a successful eight-week trial.

The time sheet used covers 70 unspecified days, with columns for starting, lunch and finishing times, and total hours worked. Each row of 10 days also has a column for proposed hours worked, and in the scheme the staff must sign in when they are ready to start work and not before. Management can easily check on staff movements, as all time sheets are kept in a central area for easy reference.

Cost of such manual recording systems are the lowest of all flexible working schemes. Printing costs for time sheets vary with the types of card used, and from printer to printer. The important factor is the principle involved. Manual recording—an 'honour' system—is compatible with the increased responsibility given to staff by the adoption of flexible working time—mechanical recording is not.

Mechanical recording : Lufthansa

Lufthansa's Cologne head office is open between 07 00 and 19 00. Core time there runs from 09 30 until 15 30. All 1,100 employees there clock in and out—even the company's chairman—and the system seems to be working well. A survey conducted in August 1971, 18 months after *Gleitzeit* was introduced there, showed that 96 per cent of all personnel like the system. Some 39 per cent of the company's managers said that their department's efficiency had increased, while 55 per cent said no change, and only 3 per cent thought it had gone down.

In Britain, as with J. Walter Thompson GmbH, there has often been considerable opposition to formal time recording, particularly with employees (like office staff) that have not previously had to clock in. Lufthansa German Airlines introduced flexible working time in its London offices on 1 January 1972, after a nine-month trial period. There was no problem in going over to clocks because of the high proportion (about 40 per cent) of Germans on the staff.

The mechanical recording system used in Lufthansa is one manufactured by the International Time Recording Co. Ltd. It consists of a main time clock, which graphically records starting and finishing times on a special card. A new time-recording card, shown in Figure 4:1, was introduced on 1 January 1973, in the interests of standardisation.

The card, which covers 31 days, is stamped by the clock for starting and finishing times only, there being no clocking out during the lunch break. The employee then fills in time worked, total time worked, hours compensated, absences and authorised overtime.

There are some 21 different symbols of absence, including: U = annual holiday, F = off days, K = sickness, B = accident at work, L = training course participation, H = paid compensating day in lieu of public holiday, and W = unpaid holiday, other absences, without pay.

The problem of showing how overtime is to be paid— 50 per cent plus time off, or at 150 per cent with no time off—has only just been solved. There are four columns on the card in the income tax section, subdivided into two 'chargeable' and two 'free' columns. The first column under 'chargeable' is filled in with the overtime hours that are to be paid at 50 per cent, i.e. the employee is expected to take an equivalent period of time off. If overtime is to be paid (at 150 per cent) the second column is completed.

Shift workers who work on Sundays have their Sunday hours paid at 50 per cent, and this is entered in the first column under 'free'. The last 'free' column covers those who work Bank Holidays and are paid at 100 per cent.

This section obviously covers shift workers whose hours are not flexible and demonstrates the flexibility of the Lufthansa development. In London, for example, the company has a cargo centre which has operators on 12-hour shifts and is open 24 hours a day. These workers do not work flexible hours, except for the accounts section, secretaries and managers. There are also reservations staff, passenger terminal staff and mechanics on 8- and 10-hour shifts whose hours are not flexible. But all the staff in administration do have flexible hours and it is likely that even telephonists will soon be working a 'staggered gliding' system.

All these different staff categories are easily accommodated

Figure 4:1   Lufthansa clock card

| 5 BA 1–3 | | |
| 1973 Month 02 10–11 | | |

To HAM PV 1

DAVIES
DIETLIND
LON BK 41

79673 H
510000   A

Name   *DAVIES DIETLIND*
PK–Nr.   *29.673 H*

1	Time worked Tägliche Anwesenheitszeit		Initial Namenskurzzeichen	Symbol of absence Abwesenheitssymbol	Total time worked Gesamtzeit	Adjust Zu/ Abschreib. Lst. Month Vormonat	Hours compensated Freizeitausgleich		Authorized overtime Angeordnete Mehrarbeit		Night hours	To be completed by BK Vom BK auszufüllen							Month February 1973
Date Datum	In Kommt	Out Geht			Arbeitszeit			Date Datum	Hours Stunden	Approved Genehmigt	Nachtstunden	Income tax Chargeable Steuerpflichtig		Free Steuerfrei		Additional payment for nightwork Nachtzuschlag			Date Datum
												%	%	%	%	%	%		
1	7.50	5.05	VR	VR	7.55	+4.35	yes/no												1
2	9.00	4.90	kaputt	kaputt	7.90		yes/no												2
3					F		yes/no												3
4					F		yes/no												4
5	9.15	5.35			8.20		yes/no												5
6	8.85	5.20			8.35		yes/no												6
7	8.70	5.60			8.90	–.25	yes/no												7
8	8.90	5.00			8.10		yes/no												8
9	8.80	4.85			9.05		yes/no												9
10					F		yes/no												10
11					F		yes/no												11
12	9.20	5.45			9.25		yes/no												12
13	9.30	5.65			8.35		yes/no												13
14	9.00	4.70			7.70		yes/no												14
15	9.00	5.30			8.30		yes/no												15
16	9.10	4.35			7.25		yes/no												16

Carried FWD

| a | b | c | d |

| Remaining vacation 44–46 | Entitlement vacation 47–48 | Vacation for the disabled 49 | Additional vacation 50–51 |

K = Sickness
B = Accident at work
T = Accident on way to and from work
M = Inability to work on account of pregnancy
    (not applicable in U.K. & Ireland)
Y = Convalescence
E = Military service
V = Late arrival
G = Approved late arrival at work in
    accordance with Rules of Employment
    or business requirements
C = Days after termination of employment
    or apprenticeship
N = Days before commencement of employment

U = Annual Holiday
S = Special leave as per our Rules of Employment
W = Unpaid Holiday, other absences, without pay
A = Time off in lieu for overtime and work on
    Public Holidays
F = Off days (Saturday/Sunday or rostered off days)
X = Unnotified absences
L = Training course participation
R = Duty travel journey and other official absence
H = Paid compensating day in lieu of Public Holiday
J = Temporary or permanent transfer abroad
I = Off days in accordance with or shift rosters during
    periods covered by symbols K, B, T, M, Y, or E

The symbols listed below are to indicate days of absence from work (whole days only).
Each day of absence should be recorded by the competent administrative unit in red.

To be completed by BK
Vom BK suszufüllen

Date Datum	Time worked Tägliche Anwesenheitszeit		Initial Namenskurzzeichen	Symbol of absence Abwesenheitssymbol	Total time worked Gesamt Arbeitszeit	Adjust Zu/ Abschreib. Lst. Month Vormonat	Hours compensated Freizeitausgleich	Date Datum
	In Kommt	Out Geht						
	Brought FWD Übertrag				96.90	74.10		
28 17							yes/no	
29 18	F				F		yes/no	
30 19	61 895	61 5 30			F		yes/no	
31 20	02 910	02 5 90			9.36		yes/no	
32 21	12 940	12 5 35			8.80		yes/no	
33 22	22 895						yes/no	
41 30							yes/no	
42 31							yes/no	
43			Total for month		A	B	C	
					% 160	A + B		
						Monthly debit		
						C/F to next month		

Bearbeitungsvermerk PV 2   Lochen   Prüfen

Date Datum	Authorized overtime Angeordnete Mehrarbeit		Night hours Nachtstunden	Income tax		Free Steuerfrei		Additional payment for nightwork Nachtzuschlag	
	Hours Stunden	Approved Genehmigt		Chargeable Steuerpflichtig					
				%	%	%	%	%	
17									
18									
19									
20									
21									
22									
30									
31									

Total for month

D				Total payment
	Stundensatz Per hour			
D	Shift allowance %			
C	%			
To be paid	Night			Total

Signature of Department Manager

by the system. The cards are kept in racks alongside the clock during each working month and are sent to head office in Cologne when completed. There a computer printout covering two months is prepared. This shows, for each employee, cumulative days worked, free time taken, a running total of holidays and all the absences. Each department head knows the percentage of sickness, the amount of holidays remaining in the year, etc. and this helps to plan work loads.

The International Time Recording Company's clock costs approximately £150 installed. In Lufthansa's London office it serves 60 people, but it could take in some 200. This is a maximum because, despite flexible working hours, people still tend to use the same trains as before, and if more than 200 employees used the same clock there could be big queues.

Lufthansa's basic system could change. At present identity cards are used for a number of different functions. These cards have a computer punch down one side, and they allow employees to enter a building through locked revolving doors (for security), buy petrol and enter car parks. It's likely that by 1975 they could be used for clocking in and out.

An administrative improvement that will probably come into operation shortly is a ready-reckoning calculator of hours worked. This is a grid showing possible starting times during the flexible two hours between 07 30 and 09 30 in three-minute intervals vertically, and the flexible finishing times (between 16 00 and 18 30) in a similar manner horizontally. Then all any employee has to do is to read along the row of his starting time till it crosses the row of numbers of his finishing time and that intersection gives the number of hours worked.

Mechanical recording : Hengstler system

One mechanical recording system that has been developed especially for flexible working is the equipment which is manufactured by Hengstler Flextime Ltd. Its creator is the company's managing director, Willi Haller, who joined the old Swabian firm of J. Hengstler KG as an apprentice at 16. After working in the company (which manufactures measuring and recording instruments) for some 18 years, Haller became fired with enthusiasm for the *Gleitzeit* system developed by Messerschmitt–Bölkow–Blohm.

In 1969 he designed a time-recording machine which eliminated most of the prejudice against the traditional time clock, a piece of precision equipment specific to flexible working systems, and a new company, Hengstler Flextime, was created to manufacture and market it.

Haller's machine (Figure 4:2) consists of a clock which is connected to a series of individual counters. Each employee has a personal, plastic code key (with picture and name printed on it) which he inserts into one of the counters when he starts work. While the code key is in the slot, the clock counts up the units of time the employee works, until the key is removed. Beside the counter's slot is the employee's personal recorder, which shows the amount of time worked.

The most important feature of the system is that it does not record any starting or finishing times. It simply shows a daily cumulative total. It is for this reason that the equipment has been installed in many companies including Allen and Hanburys in Britain. There, management firmly believed that flexible working time required an equally progressive recording system—not one with the stigmas of the conventional 'clock in'.

The equipment's advantage of actually displaying an employee's current 'time account' clearly, at any time, was the main reason why it was chosen by the management of Boehringer Mannheim GmbH, a chemicals manufacturer that employs some 3,000 at its Mannheim plant. The company faced appalling traffic congestion on its one approved road, a similar problem to that which was faced by Messerschmitt–Bölkow–Blohm.

Having faced increasing severe delays to both staff and goods vehicles, despite working hours staggered in three

Figure 4 :2   Hengstler time-recording equipment with personal counter for each employee

periods, the company decided to implement a flexible working system in Spring 1969. But it faced several difficult problems in 'negotiating' the system with its employees.

Boehringer was bound by an industry-wide wage agreement, and this specified a settlement period of only three weeks. Now the normal settlement period of flexible working time is two months; working time credits being built up over an accounting period of a month, and worked off during that or the following month. This difference nearly aborted the scheme at the start. However, after 'very full' trade union discussions the wage agreement was amended, to allow for a 15 week settlement period.

The trade unions were firmly set on a credit limit. The maximum for both credit and debit times was fixed at 10 hours, and the trade unions insisted that any excess credits over 10 hours be written off. This virtually ensured that the Hengstler system was chosen—for no employee wanted to risk forfeiting any hours he might work over the permitted carry-forward limit. The Hengstler units showed each his personal account at a glance—and they were installed for a trial period in Boehringer's personnel and O and M departments on 1 September 1969. By the end of 1970, 2,000 employees were on flexible working time and now the system is extended throughout the company.

With literally thousands of companies intent on following such examples, Willi Haller of Hengstler must be credited as the main *developer* to date of flexible working time. He believes implicitly in it. 'It makes people human again,' he says. 'It is nothing less than the revolution of the working man.'

Boehringer has certainly found this to be the case—with a vast majority of its staff now insisting on flexible working, rather than fixed or staggered hours. The company's productivity has increased, time lost has been cut by some 50 per cent, accounting has been simplified and administration streamlined.

The Hengstler system's only disadvantage is its cost—but

this is an initial factor. For example, Allen and Hanburys estimate the cost of installing the equipment at about £12 per employee; operating costs thereafter are negligible. But it says that if it was to cover all of its 1,300 Ware employees by the equipment, it would recoup the capital expenditure in two years.

5

Flexible working time installed by management : Wiggins Teape Ltd

The Hengstler system inspired Wiggins Teape Ltd to be one of the first British companies to implement flexible working time. Its carefully planned trial and subsequent adoption of the system is well worth examining in detail. It is a model of practical management, and like all good applications of any system it gave rise to a development of flexible working time, tailored to suit the company's own needs, that could well be copied by other companies, to their benefit.

In October 1971, J. Hengstler Co. (Great Britain) showed its specially developed equipment at the Business Efficiency Exhibition. This, combined with a *Financial Times* article on *Gleitzeit* in Germany, inspired Lindsay Pirie, Wiggins Teape's administration services manager, to examine the potential of installing such a system in the company's head office, Gateway House in London. Together with the personnel director, and company secretary, Pirie asked his managing director if a trial could be arranged.

On getting approval, the three devised (with the aid of

Hengstler) a set of 'rules', and carefully chose a representative group of 140 staff for the trial.

For the first time, the company had to really *quantify* time. For example, what was meant by 'standard working hours', and 'overtime'? Until then, like most City business houses, the company had disregarded overtime for clerical staff.

Introducing the scheme

The Hengstler equipment was installed in Pirie's office, and over a three-week period all the trialists were invited in to see it. They were 'sold' the system individually during that time.

The introductory document, which appeared on 31 December 1971 is reproduced in Figure 5:1.

The trial started in February 1972, and in June there was a survey into its effectiveness (see Figure 5:2). Out of 143 participating in the trial, 140 asked for flextime. In addition, 88 said it increased efficiency, and 137 had no objections to the time-recording system.

A thorough study of the trial showed that the scheme did not have to be altered at all to apply it to the rest of the staff in Gateway House and the company's Croydon offices. It was necessary to avoid snowing supervisors under with time records. So a simple diary sheet was devised (see Figure 5:3).

This document, which covers a four-week period, lists the credits and adjustment for each employee. At the end of each period, each employee agrees his carry-forward hours, etc., with his boss.

Figure 5 : 1   Document issued by Wiggins Teape Ltd to employees participating in a trial of flexible working time

The company has decided that a trial of 'flextime' should take place in Gateway House early next year. Briefly, in the system, fixed times for arrival and departure are replaced by a working day split into two different types of time. The main part, when employees *must* be at their job is called 'core time'. The flexible hours are at the beginning and end of each day, so that, subject to departmental requirements, employees may decide when to arrive and leave work. Over an accounting period of four weeks, employees are expected to have worked a specified number of hours with limited provision for carry-over to a subsequent period.

Advantages
1   Bad timekeeping is eliminated. Each individual chooses his own time for starting and stopping work during the flexible hours.
2   The rush-hour crush can be alleviated by choosing your own time to travel.
3   Married women can more easily fit in their family and housekeeping responsibilities.
4   Easier recruitment—particularly of female staff.
5   During the early and late part of the day there are fewer interruptions.
6   Experience has shown elsewhere that overtime and absenteeism is reduced.
7   It is possible to arrange, with prior permission, for a half day or even a whole day off to use up credit hours.

Figure 5 :1   continued

Disadvantages
1 Some form of time counting must be provided.
2 Only between 10 00 and 16 00 instead of 09 00 and 17 00 will all staff be in the office.

It would seem that the balance is very much in favour of flextime both for the staff and the company.

February, March and April 1972 trial period
The following will participate in the trial:

Industrial Department
Overseas: Administrative Zones and Secretarial Services
Central Staff Records
Group Secretary's Office:
    Pensions Department
    Duplicating Centre
    Fourth-Floor Secretarial Services Centre

The adoption of flextime in Gateway House and Croydon will depend upon the outcome of this trial. Two criteria will be used in deciding this outcome.

1 Does flextime improve the efficiency and service given by the departments involved?
2 Does flextime find favour with the majority of the staff involved. We would determine this by asking each member of the staff involved in the trial?

Proposed rules (subject to amendment as experience dictates) are
1 The standard total of contracted hours per four-week period is 140 (pro rata for part-timers). This is the same as our present 09 00 to 17 00 less 1 hour for lunch.
2 Core time is from 10 00 to 16 00.
3 Staff may start work at any time between 08 00 and 10 00 and finish between 16 00 and 18 00 subject to the working requirements of their department. These hours are called flextime.
4 The minimum lunch break is 30 minutes, but by arrangement with the manager, staff may exceed 1 hour, this being the paid lunch interval.

Figure 5 :1   continued

5 In addition to the use of flextime for adjusting total hours worked, staff will have the privilege, with permission from their manager, of taking off two half days or one whole day per four-week period.

6 Time worked during the flextime will not normally be considered for overtime payments.

7 (a) At the end of each week a staff member may only be in credit or debit, compared with his normal contracted hours, by up to a maximum of 7 hours without the consent of his manager.

   (b) The maximum debit or credit of time that may be carried over to the next four-week period is 7 hours.

   (c) If a manager requests working which could result in an excess over the maximum 7 hours credit at the end of a four-week period, he will arrange for staff to take time off in lieu before the end of the period where possible or for the payment of overtime.

   (d) Staff will not normally be credited with time outside the 08 00 and 18 00 starting and finishing times. In exceptional circumstances a manager may request or authorise work outside these hours. This time will then rate as overtime and will be satisfied by time off or payment.

8 Time off sick or away on business will be authorised by the departmental manager as hours worked (that is 7 per day).

9 *Late trains, holdups, etc.* Because hours can be made up and staff have the advantages flextime offers, the company expects the normal hazards of transport delays to be accepted. However, if there are major holdups then time will be credited at the discretion of the manager concerned.

The rules will be reviewed during the period of the trial.

All staff will appreciate that the overriding consideration must be the completion of work. Therefore, it will not *always* be possible to take advantage of flextime on a particular day. Supervisors will need to ensure that some members of their staff are present between 09 00 and 17 00.

Figure 5 :1   continued

Examples

Period 1	Hours
Opening balance	0
Hours worked	150
Aggr. hours	150
3 hours authorised overtime	
7 hours credit fwd	

Period 2	
Opening balance	+ 7
Hours worked	131
Aggr. hours	138
2 hours debit fwd	

Period 3	
Opening balance	− 2
Hours worked	145
Aggr. hours	143
3 hours credit fwd	

Period 4	Hours
Opening balance	+ 3
Hours worked	146
Aggr. hours	149
No overtime authorised	
7 hours credit fwd	

Period 5	
Opening balance	+ 7
Hours worked	138
Aggr. hours	145
5 hours credit fwd	

Period 6	
Opening balance	+ 5
Hours worked	145
Aggr. hours	150
3 hours authorised overtime	
7 hours credit fwd.	

The examples above are shown, for sake of clarity, to whole numbers of hours. In fact, a recording system would work in fractions of an hour.

Figure 5 : 2 Attitude survey by Wiggins Teape

Department	Like		Efficiency			Objections to timing	
	Yes	No	Less	Same	More	Yes	No
Audio (1st Floor)	3	—	—	2	1	—	3
Secretary's Office (5th Floor)	13	1	1	7	6	—	14
Pensions Department	7	—	—	6	1	—	7
Central Staff Records	6	—	—	6	—	—	6
Industrial Department	28	1	2	10	17	4	25
Overseas Administration	71*	2*	4	14	54	1	71
Secretarial Services	12	—	—	3	9	1	11
Total	140	4	7	48	88	6	137

* One ballot paper voted Yes and No.

Figure 5 :3   Example of a Wiggins Teape diary sheet

Name ___**A.N. OTHER**___   Week 1   Adjustment hours

                                    M_____

4 week period : ___**W/E 29.9.72**___   T____**3 hrs**____   CROYDON

                                    W_____

_____   Th_____

                                    F_____

Standard hours   ___140___   Week 2

                                    M_____

                                    T_____

Total adjustment hours ___8___   W_____

                                    Th____**2 hrs**____   FORGOT KEY

Revised standard hours ___132___   F_____

                                    Week 3

                                    M_____

Actual hours on clock   ___135___   T_____

                                    W____**7 hrs**____   AWAY SICK

                                    Th_____

Brought forward
from last month   ___CREDIT 3___   F_____

                                    Week 4

To be carried forward
to next month   ___CREDIT 6___   M_____

                                    T_____

                                    W_____

                                    Th_____

                                    F_____

                                    Total adjustment hours =

Installing the complete scheme

After the successful trial, and subsequent development of the diary sheet, the board confirmed that flextime should be adopted in its Gateway House and Croydon offices, where appropriate. The next stage was a comprehensive document on the scheme, sent to all staff (even those already on flextime) in October 1972.

The first part of this document was virtually a copy of the introductory document. The second part gave the results of the survey. The third detailed the company's policy on over-time payments. This is reproduced in Figure 5:4.

Flexible working hours are now enjoyed by some 400 staff in Gateway House and another 200 in Wiggins Teape's Croydon offices—to such an extent that Lindsay Pirie says: 'We can honestly say we haven't had any problems. If we tried to revert to standard working, we'd have a mutiny on our hands.'

Unjustified suspicions

Initially there were fears about the system. First, there was the fear that an employee would insert another's key in the system, 'covering up for him'. This has never occurred.

A second fear was that an employee might cheat by leaving his key in at lunchtime—instead of 'clocking out'. However this does not happen because the machines are in the depart-ment, and staff do not like to see others cheat.

The third fear was that a boss and his secretary would want to work at different times. However, many secretaries have been working flexibly for years—taking longer lunch-breaks when the boss is on a trip, and so on.

Finally, there was a fear that everyone in a department might want the same time off—for Christmas shopping for example. However, in practice there is no problem because people have very different patterns of behaviour.

The clear lessons from the Wiggins Teape success are:

1 Have a trial period.
2 Do not try to give everyone flexible working hours too soon.
3 Above all, get the managing director's total coöperation.

Figure : 5 : 4   Extract from Wiggins Teape manual for flexible working

---

Salaries
Salary scales are based on a standard 35-hour working week.

Overtime
The company believes that overtime working by staff is undesirable and that the work of staff should be organised so that overtime is minimised.

Staff earning up to £2,316 per annum
1 Any overtime worked must be authorised by department managers before commencement.
2 When essential overtime is worked, department managers may compensate the member of staff by time off in lieu or, if this is not possible, authorise payment at the following rates:
Overtime worked Monday to Saturday inclusive—

one and a half times the appropriate hourly rate $\dfrac{\text{annual salary}}{52 \times 35}$

Overtime worked on Sundays or Bank Holidays—
at twice the appropriate hourly rate
3 Payment may only be authorised in units of one hour or more.
4 For part-time staff, payment for all hours worked in excess of their normal working hours will be at 'plain rate' up to 35 hours and thereafter as above.

Staff earning over £2,316 per year
1 Overtime payment will not normally be made to such staff although in exceptional cases department heads may authorise

this after obtaining approval from Group Personnel Services Department.

2   Hours in excess of 35 will, wherever possible, be compensated by time off in lieu.

Payment
Payment is made monthly on written authority from department managers direct to Salary Calculations Department for Gateway House and G.A.D. and Cashiers other staff at Croydon.

Exceptions
Certain staff members are covered by special arrangements. The rules laid out above do not apply to:

> Mailing Room staff
> Hall Porters.

6

Flexible working time installed by joint committee : Pilkington Brothers Ltd

Cooperation and total commitment to the system, at all levels from top management down, have been the hallmarks of another British flexible working pioneer—Pilkington Brothers. Its scheme, very different from, yet as well planned as, Wiggins Teape's, stemmed from the staff consultative committee at its research and development laboratories at Lathom in Lancashire.

The Lathom site, some 12 miles from the group's headquarters in St Helens, is approached only through narrow country roads. So staff suffered the same irritating traffic congestion problems that stimulated Messerschmitt–Bölkow –Blohm to develop *Gleitzeit*. Hearing of MBB's system, Manfred Landau, manager of Pilkington's chemistry department at Lathom, visited MBB and then reported his findings on the system to Lathom's staff consultative committee.

This committee consists of Landau, plus the head of the services research department and six research workers. Six months after its initial decision to explore flexible working, a pilot scheme was implemented, in October 1971, which involved members of the service, technology and engineering departments.

Pilot scheme

A steering committee was set up. The staff were involved from the very beginning. The system was explained to them and a list of provisional rules was issued. The next step was a general meeting. Virtually everyone there who was eligible for the pilot scheme voted in favour, though individuals were allowed to opt out if they insisted.

The Pilkington system is a much modified version of MBB's. First, the rules of the scheme laid down four basic principles:

1   That the work of the department must not suffer
2   That staff concerned should not lose any previously enjoyed privileges
3   That the scheme should include volunteers only
4   That a department's participation is contingent on its manager's approval.

The hours of work are quite straightforward: a flexible starting band between 07 00 and 09 00; fixed hours 09 00–12 00; a flexible lunch break ($\frac{1}{2}$ hour minimum, $1\frac{1}{2}$ hour maximum) between 12 00 and 14 00; fixed hours between 14 00 and 16 00; and a flexible finishing band between 16 00 and 19 00.

For the pilot scheme, and subsequently, arrangements were made to provide extended cover for other essential services such as keys, library and copying facilities. Sections were told to ensure that, wherever possible, where service work was concerned, cover be provided for 'normal' hours, i.e. 08 30 to 17 00.

Time recording

Time recording was regarded as 'essential', and the steering committee proposed a clock/clock-card system. This was agreed by the staff, the clock being seen not in the image of a watchdog, but as a standard, unbiased and permanent means of time recording. The clocks are sited as near as possible to the place of work.

The clock cards, mounted in racks beside the clocks, also serve as in/out indicators (being transferred to the relevant racks when an employee enters or leaves the building). At the end of each week they are collected, inspected for legibility and passed to the computer department.

The subsequent printouts, showing time credits and debits, the amount of sick leave, holidays taken, etc. then go directly to section heads for 'display and distribution'.

Instructions to staff

The 'guidelines' laid down for the pilot scheme were extremely comprehensive. They take into account credit leave, work off site, other absences, overtime, holidays, and even forgetfulness. They can certainly aid other managements in British industry develop their own approach to flexible working.

They started by setting certain limits to flexibility:

> Where the nature of the work done by a section means that cover has to be provided between 08 30 and 17 00 to deal with urgent work problems, it is the manager's responsibility to ensure that it is maintained.
>
> Where staff form members of a team or section who depend on one another's presence for working efficiently, the members must agree on the monthly hours to be adopted by the team.
>
> The increased safety risks should be borne in mind.

Section heads must ensure that anyone doing work alone is capable of doing it safely, and that potentially dangerous work is only undertaken when others are on hand.

A credit or debit of up to 10 hours can be carried forward each month. The standard working day is $7\frac{1}{2}$ hours. Normally any credit time in excess of 10 hours at the end of any four- or five-week accounting period is lost.

Accumulated credit time can be used in half- or one-day units—up to a maximum of six in an accounting period. But credit time cannot be used to take off more than two consecutive half-days (Fridays and Mondays being considered consecutive). When taking credit time in this way, as with holidays, the compulsory half-hour lunch break no longer applies. The half-day can start or finish at any time within the flexible lunch period.

One problem which the steering committee felt would cause some trouble—that of introducing the staff to clocking in and out—never materialised. But it was felt that a means of incorporating handwritten entries on clock cards was necessary to maintain a flexible and efficient scheme.

In line with this, a series of code numbers were drawn up, to cover different absence situations. Code numbers are:

- 1: Used when absent for a half-day or longer for any reason other than carried-forward credit leave. Examples are business, conference, etc.
- 2: Used when taking a half-day from carried-forward credit leave. The code must be repeated if two successive half-days are taken for credit.
- 3: Used when payment is to be made for authorised overtime before 08 30 hours, and must be accompanied by the department manager's signature.
- 4: As − 3, above, for authorised overtime after 17 00 hours.
- 5: Sickness.
- 6: Holiday.

Handwritten entries require authorisation by the section head or department manager and in most cases this can be verbal. The guidelines say:

> A handwritten entry may be inserted in the column for manual entries on the card. *A time, in 24-hour notation, and a day should be written in under the time column* with a brief explanation alongside. When the entry is being used to exclude a time period from the scheme— for example, for overtime for which payment is to be claimed—or to obtain a standard amount of credit time— for example, for holidays, sickness or time in lieu—*an appropriate code and a day should be written in under the time column.* In the latter case for the first entry a standard half-day (3.75 hours) will be credited during processing and this will be assumed to repeat until the next entry appears.
>
> Handwritten entries need not fit into chronological order as the computer program will be designed to sort the entries.

Work visits, conferences etc.

If the visit occurs within a work period, no action is needed beyond transferring the card from the 'in' rack to the 'out' rack on leaving and the reverse on returning.

If the visit extends beyond the beginning or end of a period, at the first opportunity the time should be written in, including if appropriate a lunch break.

If the visit extends to more than one day the appropriate code -1, giving credit for standard days of $7\frac{1}{2}$ hours should be written in and a written explanation added.

If the starting or finishing time falls outside the flexible-hour limits and it can be justified then the full time spent should be entered on the card and that part falling outside the flexible limits, since it does not count towards credit time, will be transferred to a separate store during processing.

Authorised absences
Sickness, doctor, dentist, optician visit etc.
If the absence covers a full work period the appropriate code, − 5, should be entered on the card either by the person concerned or his section head.

If the absence only covers part of a period the time 08 30 or 17 00, as appropriate, should be inserted in the normal column of the card.

Time in lieu
Where a department manager has authorised time in lieu for work done outside the flexible-hour limits the manual entries of time and day should be entered in the appropriate column. *This should be initialled by the authorising manager.*

Overtime
Company regulations govern overtime payment for work done outside normal hours. When such work is specifically requested by a department manager and payment for overtime is being claimed then such time cannot form part of the flexible-hours scheme and the manual entry of the appropriate code − 3 or − 4, and day code should be used. *This insertion must be supported by the authorising manager's initials.*

Holidays
If time is taken from the holiday entitlement the appropriate code − 6 and day code should be entered.

Bank Holidays
No action will be necessary. These will be allowed for automatically.

Day release
Where day release is given to attend a course the appropriate code − 1 and day code should be entered, giving $7\frac{1}{2}$ hours credit.

Forgetfulness

It is essential that there should be an even number of time entries on the card for each day for processing. Should one be missing through a lapse of memory it should be added at the first opportunity.

Finally, the guidelines to the pilot project gave all trialists the opportunity to opt out. Those who felt unable to participate could opt out, as could those who started the trial and felt unable to continue. In fact, no one did.

In the first week, the lunch-time flexible band was changed from $1\frac{1}{2}$ hours to 2 hours.

Results of the trial

The steering committee administered and monitored the pilot scheme throughout. It consisted of Manfred Landau, plus the head of group services and some six to eight staff members. During the trial it met each Monday to 'examine the previous week's cards for mistakes and inconsistencies, to assess whether modifications were necessary to the system and to evaluate the administrative capability required'.

It determined the effects of the system in three ways. It held informal individual or group discussions to probe the feelings of all trialists. Next it conducted an attitude survey (in February 1972).

This showed 100 per cent in favour of flexible working, with 80 per cent believing it increased morale, 52 per cent that it increased responsible attitude among staff, and 40 per cent that it increased efficiency.

Meetings were also held by the committee with section heads and department managers to discuss the effects of the system on work. Finally, statistical information on starting, finishing and lunch-times was collated at monthly intervals.

The avergage of results, October to February, proved to be very interesting. The average time of arrival is shown in

Figure 6 :1   Pilkington Brothers survey : average time of arrival
Average of results for October to February

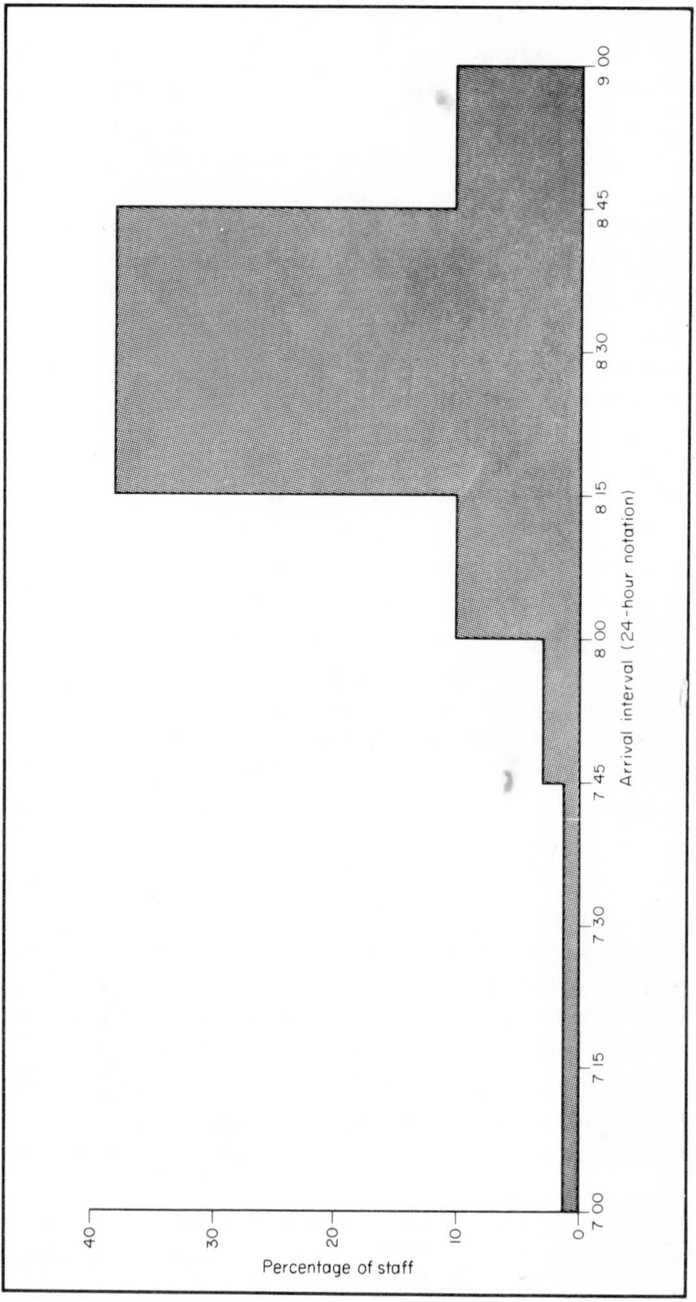

Figure 6 :2   Pilkington Brothers survey : average time of departure
Average of results for October to February

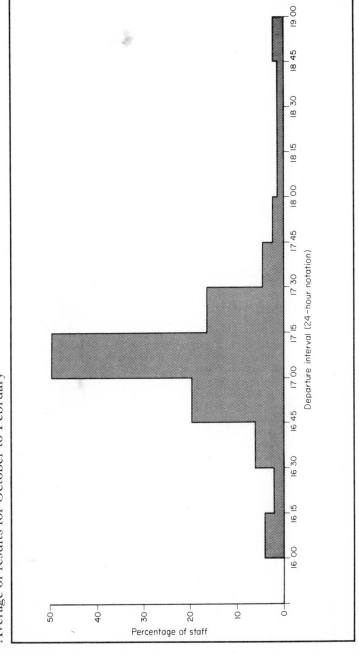

Figure 6 :3   Pilkington Brothers survey : Length of lunch interval
Average of results for October to February

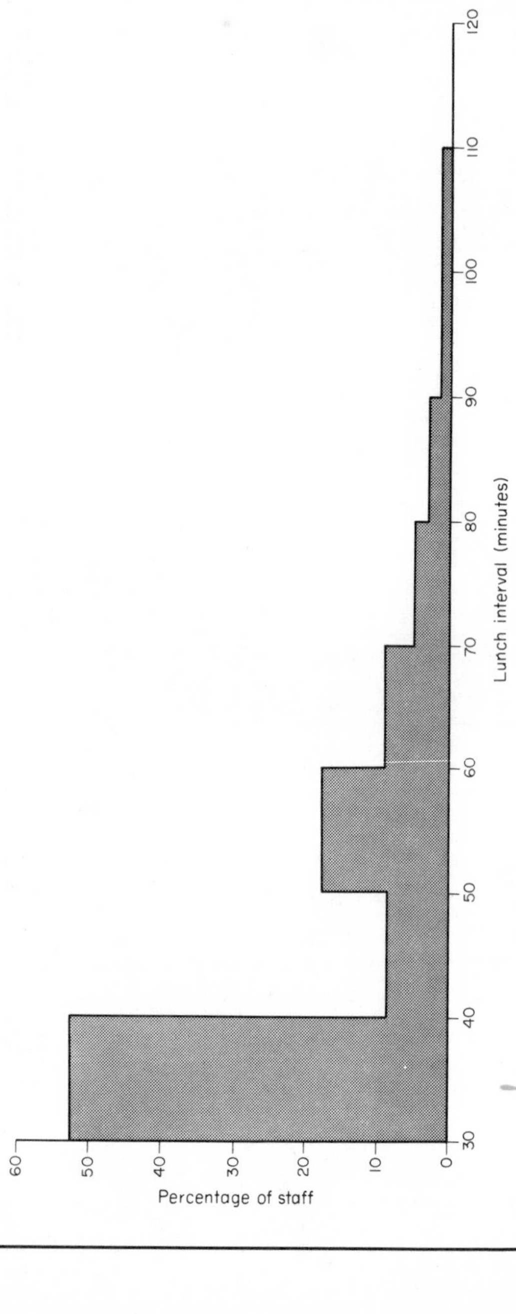

Figure 6:1. Some 2 per cent of staff clocked in in each 15 minute period between 07 00 and 07 45, 4 per cent between 07 45 and 08 00, 10 per cent between 08 00 and 08 15, 40 per cent between 08 15 and 08 30 and another 40 per cent between 08 30 and 08 45. Finally some 10 per cent arrived between 08 45 and 09 00.

Departure times (Figure 6:2) showed strange 'peaks': 5 per cent between 16 00 and 16 15, 20 per cent between 16 45 and 17 00; 50 per cent between 17 00 and 17 15 and 17.5 per cent between 17 15 and 17 30.

The result of this 'scatter' has been that traffic congestion definitely eased. But parking, perversely, proved more difficult. The committee noted, in an interim report, 'the total involvement of Lathom with flexible working hours would increase car-parking requirements by up to 10 per cent.'

The lunch-time statistics (Figure 6:3) were also significant. The previous lunch break was one hour. With flexible working a sizeable percentage (54 per cent) of staff voluntarily shortened the lunch break to 30 minutes—the minimum allowed. Only some 15 per cent took advantage of a lunch break longer than an hour during the period.

With such positive results to productivity (much of Lathom's expensive capital equipment being more productive by being used over a longer period) the 'experiment' has been slowly extended, in three stages, over a period of six months. Some 365 employees are now included and a current reappraisal could mean that all of the Lathom employees (another 200) are working flexibly in the near future.

The steering committee believes the scheme it has developed is one of the most flexible in operation. But it is not imposing it in any department, as it feels that both staff and department managers must be in full agreement before it is installed.

It is convinced that individuals are the best judges of how to pace themselves. The man doing the job is the one to say what time is likely to be wasted. Also, the man who is not pressed, rushed into missing breakfast, or subjected to a guilty conscience by being late, is far more likely to really contribute to a team's performance.

Finally, it says, 'Flexible working is something that will inevitably be adopted in the future, and management have the choice of leading towards a situation which they have helped to create, or being compelled to accept something not to their liking.'

7

Effects of flexible working

Given the firm belief of those companies that have adopted flexible working that the system will inevitably be adopted in the future, management must now try to set its benefits and disadvantages in perspective. Certainly the trade-union movement, throughout the world, is now considering the subject and debating its implications in depth.

Advantages to employees

The advantages of flexible working for an employee are difficult to quantify. First, they should be seen in relation to 'standard' hours. The Trades Union Congress defined this 'relationship' in a document that was sent to the general secretaries of all affiliated organisations, in December 1972, for comments that its General Council would consider. It says:

> The reasons given for fixed starting and finishing times are numerous: the requirements of a production process, ease of supervision, the interdependence of workers as a

result of specialisation in an integrated work situation, or the provision of heating, lighting or other services. In many cases, however, these reasons are given to justify an existing practice that owes more to custom and practice than to proven requirements.

The disadvantages of rigid work times are familiar also: congestion of roads and transport services, difficulties caused by a mismatch of the commitment to be at work at a particular hour, and domestic needs, cost of checking late arrivals and its repercussions on workers, and unpaid overtime for some salaried workers. Furthermore the practice of rigid work time has the flavour of an authoritarian attitude towards the worker, which is not acceptable particularly as the technical need for rigidity has been shown in many cases to be absent or exaggerated.

For employees, the benefits of flexible working are only really judged by the attitudes of those who have tried the system out. They admit to enjoying better travelling and working conditions, higher 'morale', more job satisfaction and the ability to take credit hours as additional leave. None of these benefits must be understated.

No one has yet quantified just how much improvement there has been in travelling conditions for those employed with flexible working hours, but there is a universal feeling that travelling is improved.

More than time, though, the relief from rush-hour tension is almost tangible to many. This might seem purely a social advantage, but many employees, including Pilkington's steering committee, are convinced that relief from such pressure contributes to a much greater degree of job satisfaction and performance.

As for morale, with no need to invent a cancelled train (as one cannot be late under the system) nor a dying grandmother (if one wants to watch football one afternoon) and given the greater responsibility of deciding when a job should be finished, clearly it is individually improved. Basic human metabolism is a root factor—some individuals work best first thing in the morning, many others pick up strength as the sun wanes. With flexible working, both types are able to work when they are near the optimum points for effectiveness—and this certainly boosts the pride in work well done felt by *every* employee.

That employees respond to these 'intangible' benefits, there is no doubt. The evidence of attitude surveys is overwhelming. At Wiggins Teape, out of 143 'trialists', 140 voted for flexible working hours. A higher percentage (33 employees out of 34) showed similar enthusiasm at Pakcel Convertors. In spite of strict rules at the ICI engineering department and instrument development group some 61 per cent were in favour. Finally, at Allen and Hanburys 100 per cent endorsed the system, and some 65 per cent said it had directly improved their working conditions.

Some disadvantages to employees

Disadvantages, generally, relate to the interaction of groups, rather than to individual staff.

For example, in some small departments (as at Wiggins Teape, where in one unit only some six staff are involved) a manager has had to limit the degree of flexibility allowed. Departments must always be manned by a minimum (in this case two) staff, and this restriction can cause resentment.

Similarly with teams of staff, complete flexibility cannot be allowed, or else the team would never function. In these cases, in many companies, teams have been allowed to choose common 'flexible' starting and finishing times—and such arrangements have worked well. But they are a possible source of friction.

Willi Haller of Hengstler sees the ultimate acceptance of flexible working hours throughout industry as depending on the principle of group working. At Bosch in Watford, the telephonists worked flexible times by agreeing the hours among themselves. This also happened with production workers at Riker Laboratories, the Loughborough pharmaceutical factory. It is almost inconceivable that flexible working hours could be applied to the motor industry as it is today. It could be argued that for full efficiency the group-working principle pioneered by Philips, Saab and Volvo should be adopted and this would also allow the adoption of flexible working hours.

Of more importance is the safety element. In some companies, there is a high element of danger if individuals work by themselves under difficult processing or experimental conditions. At Pilkington Brothers, for example, the rule is that staff may not carry out 'dangerous' work alone in the laboratories. The flexible bands must be used for desk work, until the time comes when all staff are on flexible working hours, so that safety staff can 'cover' the whole of the flexible periods.

Advantages to management

Advantages to management of flexible working systems are quite quantifiable—in terms of a definite reduction in absenteeism and overtime, and a positive increase in productivity.

To start with Messerschmitt–Bölkow–Blohm claims that since it invented *Gleitzeit,* days lost through illness and short-term absenteeism have been cut by more than 50 per cent. Minutes and hours also count—and can cost companies considerable money. The Losenhausen Maschinenbau factory reports that before implementing *Gleitzeit,* some 55 employees (10 per cent of the work force) were late every day. Within two months of starting the system, 'lateness' being eliminated, almost all short-term absences also disappeared.

The savings in terms of cash has been calculated by some. Lufthansa, for example, estimates that it has saved about £500,000 per year from gleaning 'lost days and hours'. One of the company's subsidiaries, Lufthansa Service GmbH, has also quantified its cuts in overtime.

Employing some 120 staff at its Frankfurt airport headquarters, the company had to pay a high overtime rate to central and local administrative, and maintenance staff, who were responsible for preparing meals for, and servicing, aircraft. In the three months prior to the introduction of *Gleitzeit* in May 1970, total overtime hours averaged 895 per month. This was reduced dramatically to an average of 317 hours over the next three-month period.

Losenhausen Maschinenbau also saw a considerable cost saving: overtime payments running at £80,000 in 1970 fell to £35,000 in 1971 once *Gleitzeit* was implemented. Although some 10 per cent of the workforce were lost by 'natural wastage' during the period, the firm's turnover rose from £4 million to £5.3 million.

Another quantifiable area is that of credit and debit carry forward. A possible source of problems if too many employees have too much debit time each month, it is also an advantage to management if employees stay 'in the black', as equipment is far more productive if used over a longer period.

In fact the universal tendency is to build up credit hours. Messerschmitt, for example, has an average monthly carry forward of 14,000 hours (an average of four per employee). Commerzbank AG of Düsseldorf, which started a *Gleitzeit* trial in September 1971 involving 200 staff, reported that more than 80 per cent of them were in credit throughout the period. In Britain, the trialists at Allen and Hanburys have been in credit to an average of $1\frac{1}{2}$ hours each, and none has exceeded the permissible debit limit of five hours.

The statistics of hours flexibly worked can be useful to management in other ways. If a department regularly has to work longer-than-contracted hours, this shows up clearly in the records. Management can then recruit more staff, or balance and budget its overtime payments more satisfactorily.

The TUC's provisional document, in one way, sums up the advantages to management:

A change to flexible working hours provides an employer with an opportunity to improve the efficiency of the use of both capital and labour resources. In the case of capital resources, improved efficiency is achieved by extending the available hours over which the fixed assets of the company are utilised in a productive capacity. The opportunity to improve the efficiency of the use of capital resources can only be fully realised if the pattern of the starting and finishing times of the employees is spread over the entire 'band time'. For example, if the 'band time' is 08 00 to 18 00, it would not lead to the more efficient assets if all save a few workers decided to start work at 08 00 and finish at 16 00. Under these circumstances the stem loses its 'flexibility' and resembles a staggered working day.

In practice, however, experience in the actual cases of firms using flexible working hours has shown that patterns of starting and finishing times produce a viable situation from the employer's point of view, because the 'early' and 'late' starters tend to balance out. Even so most employers will reserve the right to influence the choice of work times if the pattern becomes inconvenient. This may be merely a matter of consultation with workers, giving workers with the longest service first choice of working hours, or some similar method.

The value to employers of the increased efficiency of their fixed assets is, however, marginal when compared with the value of improved labour productivity which flexible working hours provides. In many cases flexible working time is introduced in areas of work where the workers are on 'staff' conditions and financial penalties on workers for lateness or occasional absence from work are not generally imposed. The potential output of the workforce is therefore not realised.

Also in many cases, these 'lost hours' of output, which may be made up by the employees, are usually worked outside the normal hours of work and are paid at overtime rates of pay; therefore the costs of output are out of proportion to the volume of output. One course open to management to rectify this situation would be to re-impose financial penalties for lateness and occasional absence. This course of action would obviously be not acceptable to the trade unionists concerned.

Another course would be to insist that employees make up 'lost hours of output' at two-thirds of the standard rate of pay and to impose a set of disciplines to ensure that this occurs. Flexible working time provides the employer with these disciplines by requiring the employees to work a fixed number of hours a month at standard rates of pay in return for the 'freedom', for the employees, to choose (within limits) their own pattern of work time.

Disadvantages to management

The disadvantages to the employer, in the face of such positive advantages are minimal. They are: the cost of time-recording equipment, the costs of administration, and the possible necessity of providing extra lighting and heating for an 'expanded' day. All these are overwhelmed by the cost savings from reduction in absenteeism alone.

In fact there is only one case, so far, of a company carrying out a trial of flexible working hours and abandoning (after three months) the system, that of Messer Griesheim GmbH.

The trial was held in the administration section of its industrial gas division in Düsseldorf, during 1 January to 1 April 1969—the 'work band' stretching from 07 15 to 17 30 and covering an eight-hour working day for each employee. The division handles the industrial gas sales of some 28 plants and their maintenance, so Düsseldorf staff have to be readily available.

This last factor was one which strongly influenced the decision to abandon flexible working hours. It was not possible at *all* times to reach an engineer for information, or a competent official for a decision. The management also felt that many main-office staff used the system without responsibility, taking free time without observing business essentials. It also originally believed that staff would use 'credit' hours for all private business (seeing doctors, hairdressers, etc.) but it believed in the end, that staff still used 'official working time' for these purposes.

Time credits, in fact, proved a headache. The trial system allowed staff to take a free day *within the same, or next, week* if enough credits were built up. Management then grumbled that subsequently 'some employees were officially authorised to stay away from the office for one or two days in the following week'.

Finally, Messer Griesheim found the expense of evaluation and control of time sheets 'enormous'. Although the main office has only 300 employees which is not too big, control required one person full-time.

Now all main office staff are back on fixed time. It is a pity for them and the company that a different variation of *Gleitzeit* was not tried. For it seems, in this one case, that Griesheim's management suffered only disadvantages and saw none of the many advantages of flexible working.

TUC's view of limitations

A final, thoughtful summing up of 'difficulties and limitations', rather than disadvantages, is made in the TUC's draft document on flexible working hours. Covering seven main points, it says:

> Flexible working time is most effective when individual workers are responsible for activities that do not require the presence of others. This is the situation in many fields of employment in offices and services, and in some aspects of work in manufacturing industry. However, a frequently found situation in manual jobs is one

in which a department of the factory as a whole is closely integrated in its activities. This is typical of flow production and process industries and it is true of many batch-production arrangements.

In such situations the 'core time' coincides with the 'band time' or at least represents a big proportion of it. Thus the scope for individual flexible work time is absent or is much reduced. Even in these cases, however, it may be possible to adapt the general principles of flexible working hours for groups of workers, so that some flexibility is possible on a collective rather than an individual basis. However the larger the group the less is the scope for individual choice, and then all that is different from the old system is a change of starting and finishing time for everyone.

In some firms the situation may exist in which FWT can be used for some categories of workers but not for others. For instance it might be applicable to the office but not to the works. In these circumstances the use of the scheme for one group could cause resentment by that group or by the rest of the workers because the different conditions of employment applicable to each group had been accentuated. There has been at least one case reported of a claim for compensating payments because one group of workers were excluded for technical reasons from a flexible-working scheme introduced in their establishment.

In some instances FWT could have an effect on take-home pay by reducing overtime and substituting time off in lieu of premium payments for additional hours worked. This result would not necessarily be objectionable to all trade unionists, but it is a point that needs to be taken into account. Of course, there is no reason why overtime premiums should not be applied to extra time worked at the request of the employer, and in such cases these hours would be regarded as outside the scheme, and would not be counted as credits.

Moreover, many workers in 'staff' jobs do not receive overtime pay for extra time put in to complete urgent jobs such as preparing a report at the end of the day. Numerous hours are 'given' to the employer, in odd ten minutes and half-hours, in such circumstances. A system of working time ensures that they are recorded and contribute to the worker's credits.

On the other hand it should be noted that the occasional time off taken by a worker for such purposes as visiting a dentist or a doctor is granted by some employers, especially to staff workers, without loss of pay. Unless this point is specifically established the change-over to FWT could mean that such absences would be recorded: they would in effect be taken during the worker's time and not during the employer's time. Thus FWT could mean that the employee spends more time at work.

The limitation of the number of credits that can be carried forward from month to month is introduced as a safeguard to the employer. He does not want to find that half of his staff is absent during the summer or around Christmas time because they have accumulated large numbers of credits. The limitation can also be a safe guard to workers against pressure to extend holidays at the expense of increasing the length of the working week.

It would not be in the workers' interests to secure two weeks extra holiday at the cost of increasing the working week: the need at the present time is to reduce the working year by reducing the working week and increasing holidays. (British workers have a longer working week and fewer days holiday than is the case in many other industrialised countries.)

The suggestion is sometimes made that the working week should be concentrated into four days instead of five: that there should be 'flexi-days' as well as 'flexi-hours'. The four-day week is in being in a number of firms in the USA and Canada, but in general the number of hours worked a week is less than in the UK. This fact helps to underline the point that FWT is attractive only when the length of the working week is reasonably short.

The point can be illustrated by imagining what would have been the scope of flexible working time, even on a six-day week basis, when the normal working week was 54 hours or more. This would have given a working day of 9 hours or 10 hours including a one-hour lunch break. The 'band-time' would have to have been 12 hours to have permitted even one hour flexibility, on either side of the standard time, in the starting time.

On a five-day basis, 40 hours is probably the maximum number of hours acceptable for flexible working, and many trade unionists would take the view that the first priority should be to reduce this number to 35 hours or less. It is not surprising that FWT has spread most rapidly in this country in cases where the working week is 35 hours.

8

Four-day, forty-hour week

'The switch from conventional working has generally meant civilised commuting out of rush hours, a more responsible, enthusiastic workforce, lower turnover of skilled staff, less absenteeism, and higher productivity. Costs of production, and overheads, have dropped significantly.' All these factors apply to flexible working—but the statement in fact refers to another 'work system' that has recently generated considerable interest: the four-day week.

Like flexible working the four-day week is at an 'early' development stage. The 'standard' system consists of four consecutive 10-hour days being worked in each week— leaving employees to enjoy the 'benefits' of a 'bank holiday' weekend 52 times a year. Usually companies remain open from 08 30 until 18 30 Mondays to Thursdays inclusive, although in some cases Tuesdays to Fridays are worked.

The ideas of short work schedules is scarcely new, but the formulation of four days, 40 hours into a concept, or system, occurred in America. Its originator (though not inventor) was Mrs Riva Poor, who runs a consultancy in Cambridge, Massachusetts. In 1970 she found the 4/40 week being applied in a local company, tracked down 27 other companies using the same system and published her analysis on them as 'a revolution in work and leisure'.

Her book *Four Days, Forty Hours* became a runaway best seller. It must certainly be credited with awakening real management interest in the system—previously dismissed as a passing fad, but now undoubtedly a relentless trend. By the end of 1971 more than 700 companies were working four-day weeks and Mrs Poor estimates that there are now more than 2,000, with two companies 'converting' every day, in America alone.

Mrs Poor has been described by *Newsweek* as 'the High Priestess of the four-day movement' but she denies that she is more than an analyst of an important innovation'.

Mrs Poor claims that four-day working gives real benefits to both management and workforce. Employees gain a three-day weekend for nothing. The company gains in many ways: higher productivity, lower absenteeism, easier recruitment and much improved customer and labour relations.

The big plus is that with four-day working employers schedule the *week* to fit the *work*, instead of traditionally planning production to fit the conventional five-day week. Many have found that working the same hours, but one day less per week is much more efficient.

Four-day working in Britain

Efficiency, however, in this context spells redundancy to many managements and staff. It is possibly for this reason that the four-day system is yet to gain real momentum in Britain. Yet while media, economists and business journals have been building up a four-day fervour in America, one British company has been quietly practising what they all preach for the last seven years—a good five years before the system was 'born' in the States.

The company is Roundhay Metal Finishers (Anodisers) Ltd, and its managing director Frank Spicer, an energetic, innovative Yorkshireman, hit on the idea of 4/40 through 'plain common sense'. In October 1965, soon after moving his works to Batley from nearby Leeds, he saw several of his 40-strong workforce waiting at a bus stop in the rain. He drove past the same queue some 15 minutes later when returning to the factory for some papers he had forgotten. 'My workers were cold, wet and miserable', he says, 'and I imagined what they felt seeing full-up buses pass by. I thought, "Why put up with that five days a week just to earn a decent wage? Why not do it just four days a week—and out of rush hours?" '

Spicer could see benefits to both employees and company in a shorter week. The workers would gain from better conditions, and more leisure. The company would save a day's fuel for the chemical vats, and possibly halt the drain of skilled Leeds workers. The next day he spoke to the workforce and suggested that instead of working from 07 55 to 16 25 five days a week, they should tack two hours onto the end of each day and only do four days a week.

The workforce agreed to give it a try. Most other people thought it outrageous, commercial suicide. But after only a month it was clear to Spicer that the experiment was an unqualified success. No one wanted to go back to five-day working, and it has never been considered since then.

The benefits of the system have been measurable. Productivity rose more than 15 per cent in the first year (as workers now only have a 30-minute lunch break and no tea break) and has risen by about 20 per cent since then, though it is now levelling off. The higher wages and bonus schemes (as most workers are on piece-rate) have meant that earnings have risen considerably, in some cases by up to 30 per cent. Overheads have been reduced: fuel and transport costs are down, and there are far fewer machinery breakdowns as maintenance staff have every Friday for repairs and general service.

As for the workforce, absenteeism is negligible (as losing a day's pay means losing a quarter of one's total earnings on a four-day week). Only two skilled men have left in the last eight years, and labour turnover (some 25 per cent when a five-day week was worked) is now about 5 per cent. Above all, the workforce seems genuinely, totally happy with the scheme.

Frank Spicer regularly conducts snap attitude surveys on the shopfloor. The replies to questions like 'What would persuade you to leave your present job and go to a company working a five-day week?' give a good guide to feelings. The answers range from 'Nothing', through '£1,000,000' to 'Double the money'.

Aside from the tangible benefits, Spicer himself is delighted with certain aspects of the scheme—client attitude being one. 'They thought us mad at first,' he says, 'but I guaranteed their production lines wouldn't be held up, and they haven't. But before four-day we were treated as an extension of their plant—always able to deliver the goods. Now, we keep their production staff on their toes.'

Roundhays has certainly proved a near perfect example of the four-day system. Much credit is due to Spicer's personal qualities—and the fact that the company is small, with only a few workers belonging to a trade union. In a more difficult industrial environment, the initial resistance at least to four-day would be considerable.

Many British companies are interested in the system. For guidance, Spicer says, 'We've worked it for nearly eight years now—and we've found no snags at all. If other companies really look at the system closely, I'm sure a great many of them would adopt it.'

Canadian experience

The system is being increasingly adopted in many countries outside America and Britain—in Australia, Canada, Germany, Holland, Japan and New Zealand mainly. The experience of companies in these countries has been quantified to a certain degree by specific surveys. In Canada, for example, management consultants Samson, Bellair, Riddell, Stead Inc undertook a national survey at the end of 1971 and 152 Canadian companies participated.

Of these, 100 had between 100 and 2,000 employees, 13 employed between 5,000 and 10,000, and seven employed more than 20,000 workers. Five companies in the 5,000–10,000 employee bracket had departments working a shortened week schedule, as did three companies in the 1,000–2,000 bracket. In all, 17 (or 11.2 per cent) of participating companies had direct experience of the 4/40 routine.

All these companies, which employed some 619,826 workers in total (more than 10 per cent of the Canadian total workforce) were asked to express views on the shortened work week. The positive response was enormous: 97 companies (64 per cent) felt the system 'is a practical, viable arrangement and will gain general acceptance'. In addition, another 28 companies (18.4 per cent) felt it would be generally adopted, but *unfortunately* will take many years to implement. Only one company felt it was 'a passing fad'.

Of the 17 companies working the shortened week (with a size ranging from 15 to 9,500 employees) a total of 1,555 employees were actually enjoying the benefits of the new schedule, with total hours worked ranging from 35 to 40. Of these employees 1,288 (or 82.8 per cent) were unionised— a very high percentage.

Even more significantly, in more than 70 per cent of the 17 companies the initiative for implementing the 4/40 'concept' came from management. Despite the high number of trade-union members in the survey, the unions are not really yet in favour of the system. Their general belief is that having fought long and hard to cut the working day down to eight hours, any extra daily work should be paid at time-and-a-half—which makes the whole system uneconomical.

Australian experience

Management pessimism on just this belief was also expressed
in a similar survey carried out in Australian industry by
Sydney Technical College's School of Management. An increasing number of Australian companies are now using the
four-day week—and solving absentee and labour turnover
problems successfully with it.

Cost factors have also been important, being behind many
decisions to implement the system—like that taken at Calsil
Ltd's Sydney brick plant. There with the previous five-day
week, two shifts were worked every 24 hours, each consisting of eight hours plus two hours regular overtime. This
meant a costly closedown of the highly automated production
machinery for four hours each day.

With the new four-day 35-hour week that is being worked,
maintenance is done on a weekday (instead of a Saturday)
giving the first shift every Wednesday off, and the second
every Friday off. Employees now work six hours at standard
rate, plus three hours overtime for three days, and four hours
standard, four hours overtime on the fourth day. There is now
continuous 24-hour production during the four days, and the
plant is totally shut down during the weekend.

Despite such successful applications, however, costs and
trade-union problems seem to haunt Australian management.
In the School of Management's survey, while more than
50 per cent of manufacturing companies and 45 per cent of
service firms believed they could adapt to four-day, some
72 per cent saw unions as a major problem and 78 per cent
put costs in the problem category.

Worker and management attitudes in Britain

In Britain there is little real trade-union enthusiasm for four-
day. For the unions the prospect of a 10-hour day—an
extended day—goes against all they hold dear. 'Official'

management reaction is also not really favourable. The Confederation of British Industry is lukewarm, a spokesman has said, 'If the four-day system can be implemented without loss in profitability, employers will not object to it. But they will be reluctant to take any initiative.' Similarly, Sir Richard Powell, director general of the Institute of Directors, has said, 'The four-day week is a bad joke.'

The system in fact does have its disadvantages. The use (or misuse) of spare time, the disruption of women employees' domestic routines, and worker fatigue are problem areas. The biggest disadvantage is the uneconomic use of plant.

Fatigue

Worker fatigue after a 10-hour day is very real. This has been experienced by the staff of CGD, a leading London design consultancy, which implemented a six-month trial of four-day working in November 1971. Its system maintained the previous $37\frac{1}{2}$-hour working 'week', spread over Tuesday to Friday. Previous daily hours of 09 00 to 17 30 became 08 00 to 18 30 on those days (18 00 on Friday) with a set one-hour lunch break.

'The effect of the change was mentally and physically shattering,' says Malcolm Riddell, the company sales director. 'Staff were wandering wearily from desk to bed, completely exhausted. Now we know it takes the metabolism up to six months to adjust. With such systems, management must be considerably more tolerant—for staff will be dull, or bad tempered, until they settle down to the new routine.'

CGD's staff did, in fact, settle down—the majority being enthusiastic about the system and totally unwilling to revert to a five-day week. But their experience, matching that of most four-day companies, gives substance to fears of worker fatigue when exposed to untraditional work cycles.

British workers have even responded alarmingly to a change from their traditional shift system to a Continental style of shift working. A real jump in absenteeism 'due to sickness' (by 36 per cent) was the result of a year's trial of such a system in a large East Midlands food factory.

In 1965, a Medical Research Council report recommended that shift working should be rotated slowly, changing once a week rather than every two days as on the Continent. The report on the food factory, the first full-scale survey of the medical effects of 'rapid rotation', which was published in June 1972, underlined these beliefs.

The staff at the factory voted overwhelmingly in favour of the Continental system, after a six-month trial. But despite their approval, the system's effect on their metabolism was dramatically quantified. During the trial period, 'flu hit the East Midlands and sickness (certified by doctors) rose by 8 per cent generally. At the factory, it rose by 36 per cent, and even one-day (uncertified) absences rose by 29 per cent.

In Roundhay Metal Finishers, however, as with many four-day companies, staff have acclimatised to change after a period of time. Most say they now feel no more tired than with an eight-hour day. It is probable that change, rather than longer hours, disrupts workers' health—and with shorter hours the effects of change should be considerably lessened. This seems the next development in the four-day system.

Future developments

Frank Spicer believes he can introduce a four-day 36-hour week by 1974 without affecting production. Others think that the benefits of rescheduling the working week should be more directly shared by employees, and are experimenting with such radical concepts as a three-day, 36-hour system.

One such innovator is Liptons, the American soup manu-facturers, which implemented a 12-hour 3-day week in its New Jersey, New York and Texas plants in 1972. Workers are divided into four shifts. One works 07 00 to 19 00 Mondays to Wednesdays, another 19 00 to 07 00 on the same days. The third and fourth shifts duplicate these times Thursdays to Saturdays. All shifts have a 27-minute meal break, and four 15-minute rest breaks.

Many employees are unhappy with the system, mostly married staff with young children.

9

A system based on trust : Schreiber Wood Industries Ltd

Schreiber Wood Industries Ltd has grown during the last three years into Britain's biggest furniture manufacturer. It has also built up a reputation for a company that believes that its 2,800 employees are important people—to such an extent that a plan to go public in November 1972 was called off when the 1972 pay freeze stopped a share incentive scheme designed for the shopfloor.

At the Essex factories, employees do not have to clock on or clock off. The system is based on trust, self-policed by workmates. Overtime has been abolished, and short time with it. And the factories are 100 per cent union shops.

An indication of the growth of the company that works in this naturally flexible way can be gained from the fact that in 1962 its sales were less than £1.3 million, and pre-tax profits less than £50,000. In the year ending March 1972, however, sales totalled £14.3 million, and pre-tax profits topped £1.4 million.

A further example of the drive shown by its senior management and workforce are the results of its Harlow factory. In

1967, facing a capacity problem, the company acquired a 75 per cent stake in Greaves & Thomas Ltd. It gutted the latter's Harlow plant and replanned it on a flow-line production technique, many of the Schreiber workforce helping out in their own time. Previously the plant had turned out some £800,000 of furniture per year. It now runs in excess of £5 million a year.

Shopfloor starting-point of system

As with Frank Spicer of Roundhay, the personal energy and qualities as an employer of the company's managing director have been largely responsible for its excellent industrial environment. Chaim Schreiber, as did all but one of his top management, graduated from the shopfloor. Polish-born, having trained as an architect in Vienna until 1938, he spent six years during the war as a 'wood engineer' building Mosquitoes for the British aircraft industry. Aside from applying the techniques he developed during this period to the mass production of radio and television cabinets, and subsequently to furniture, he does see all his company's operations from the shopfloor's viewpoint.

The company's flexible work style is in fact a combination of *Mitbestimmung* (worker participation in management) and *Gleitzeit*. There really is no 'system'—which proves clearly that the most important requisite is the *attitude* of senior management.

The workforce has been on a form of flexible hours for the last three years. The 'lowest' grade of worker is classified as a 'labourer', but these constitute only 2 per cent of employees. They become servicemen very quickly, and those that show promise go on to become journeymen. There is an agreement that management need not upgrade from this category if skilled men are available outside, but they often do upgrade. The grade above journeyman is leading hand, who is responsible for a group and plans the job for the line. He cannot hire or fire, works an average 44 hours per week over the year, and keeps the line going—without overtime.

An example of the flow-line organisation is seen in the company's kitchen-unit factory at Hoddesdon, Hertford-shire. There are three production lines in operation there at the moment. Each has 26 skilled men, four women, four servicemen, a supervisor and a leading hand. In one week these three lines produce units to the value of £108,000.

None of the men clock in or out. If a man is not absent at all during a year, he gets one day off with pay for every two months. If he wants to take time off, at any time, he agrees this with his supervisor and then comes in and makes the time up when it is convenient.

Although the company has abolished overtime (in the current conventional use of the term) a man 'making up' time on Saturday mornings, for example, is allowed to *work* it off at time and a half. In other words, if he loses nine hours on a weekday, he need only work six hours on a Saturday to 'make up' those lost hours. But the system cannot be abused. If a man tries constantly to work a 35-hour week by working every Saturday morning at time-and-a-half, the shopfloor committee soon stops him.

Paid overtime is also occasionally allowed under specific circumstances. If there are work bottlenecks, the company asks certain workers to do overtime, preferably for a four-week spell. If this spell occurs in the three-month period prior to an employee's holiday, as an inducement, his holiday pay is up-graded that year to the overtime rate.

The workforce is motivated to boost the company's success, by a profit-sharing scheme. They get paid, twice a year, the equivalent of three weeks pay, at Christmas and in mid-summer. If a worker is letting the side down, the others soon put him back in line. It's in everyone's interest, so that profits and leisure can be enjoyed, that the 'system' is not abused.

But there are many other facets to the practical approach shown by the company's management. All workers have free group life assurance, worth one year's salary. On retirement (at 65) everyone gets a week's pay for every two year's service as a 'golden handshake'. Even the rewards for the company's suggestion scheme are proportionately sensible—50 per cent of what the idea saves in six months, topped by a £50 bonus.

As for the trade unions, the company *pays* the works committee to hold its meetings out of hours. (There are five committee members at Harlow, some 40 in the other factories.) Committee chairmen get paid £8 per month, stewards £2 per month. The payment is for work done out of hours—there is no question of bribery.

Role of shopfloor committee

There is also a workforce committee which examines sickness among employees. All sick workers get their total wages. The committee examines cases of suspected malingering and tells management if a man is malingering, in which case it would not allow him to be paid.

This shopfloor committee is a cornerstone of the method the company uses to control and direct its employees. Every day, the supervisors fill in a standard form which simply lists absentees, their hours lost and the reasons why (see Figure 9:1). At the end of each week, they tally up the number of hours lost, then fill in a summary sheet for each absent employee only, which also lists reasons for hours lost (see Figure 9:2).

Each week the committee examines these records (there is one committee for each of the company's factories). Each committee consists of two management representatives (usually the works manager and a foreman) and a chairman and secretary who come from, and are elected by, the shopfloor. They meet each Monday afternoon during working hours to fiinish their review in time for the computer's run of its wages program that night. (The men get paid each Thursday for the current week, but absentees, sicknesses, etc. are adjusted two weeks later.)

Schreiber Group
Weekly absenteeism/lateness record

Factory HARLOW   Section 2 MILL   Week ending 3.3.73

Important:— An employee's name must appear only once on this sheet and his total week's sickness must be recorded against this one entry

Date	Name	Clock number	Reason for absence and how notified	Hours lost	Normal weekly hours	Normal gross pay	Earnings this week	Sick pay	Pay / No
						For office use only			
²⁴/₂/73	S. FEARNE	22	FREE DAY						\
²⁷/₂/73	D. BUNES	49	SENT HOME BY NURSE 9.30 TUES	6½	40				✓
²⁷/₂/73	S. LAWLOR	109	HOSPITAL IN PATIENT	27	44				✓
²⁸/₂/73	M. OWEN	168	FREE-DAY						✓
²⁷/₂/73	T. O'DONNELL	83	HOSPITAL APPOINTMENT HARLOW	4	44				✓
²⁸/₂/73	T. MOOLD	113	FREE DAY						✓
²³/₂/73	B. ANDERSON	57	FREE DAY						✓
²⁸/₂/73	P. PAYNE	197	TWISTED KNEE AT WORK	26	44				✓
²⁸/₂/73	T. KEAST	97	SENT TO HIS OWN DOCTOR BY HEALTH SERVICE	8	40		TIME MADE UP		✓
¹/₃/73	T. KELLY	165	FREE DAY						✓
²/₃/73	S. JOHNSON	23	FREE DAY						✓
²/₃/73	M. GROSSMAN	8	FREE DAY						✓
²/₃/73	K. COLLIS	375	FREE DAY						✓
²/₃/73	MRS. GRANT		HEAVY COLD. MESS FROM. MR. DAVIS	8	40				✓

This form must be handed to the factory wages office by 9.00 am each Monday
Signature of Foreman/Supervisor_____

Figure 9 :1   Schreiber Group : weekly absenteeism/lateness record

Schreiber Group		Name			Clock number	
Absence record		ANDERSON BRIAN			149	
Week ended	Detail	Total hours	Week ended	Detail		Total hours
27.9.68	C Funeral Weds	3½✓				
21.11.69	? a.m. Tues ¾ hrs	¾✓				
27.2.70	Hosp. PM Fri 1¼ hrs	1¼✓				
13.3.70	Back trouble P.M Mon 1¼ P.M Weds ½	1¾✓				
20.3.70	1½ Weds 1½ Fri Clinic Back trouble	3¼✓				
27.3.70	H.I.H.C. P.M. Weds	1½✓				
3.4.70	H.I.H.C. Fri	1½✓				
10.4.70	C P.M. Wed	1¼✓				
17.4.70	Pleurisy S Tues - Fri	32✓				
24.4.70	Hosp App. P.M. Weds.	1½✓				
30.4.71	Private	1½ ES				
19.12		ES				
3.3.73	Free Day Mon.					

Figure 9:2   Schreiber Group : personal absence record

The shopfloor committee and the works trade-union committee are main channels of worker-management communication. 'We like to work with the trade union,' says Chaim Schreiber, 'they're a well-organised body. If at any time they want to talk to us, a meeting is arranged by simply picking up the phone. After meetings, the committees relay our discussions to the workforce.'

Other communication methods are used. Often the pay packet is used as a means to canvass employee opinion. When management wanted to abolish clocking in they asked the men to fill in a questionnaire included in their pay packets. All the factories agreed to abolish time clocks, except the Harlow plant. The decision was not forced and they did not stop clocking in until six months later.

Schreiber firmly believes that his style of management of flexible working can be adopted by any company, regardless of size. 'Even corporations like General Motors', he says, 'consist of a number of "small" units. The most important thing is for top management to be *seen* on the shopfloor. Second, you must give your workers your trust. You must believe that anyone who is prepared to spend 40 hours a week for life in a factory or office is honest. You need no time clocks. Finally, you must get your middle management to believe this. If they're not *convinced* that employees are really responsible people, it won't work.'

The responsible treatment of the workforce in Schreiber Industries is clearly reciprocated. They have never had a single strike and on more than once occasion when a production line has had to be rejigged while the men were on holiday, many of them have turned up to help out *in their own time*.

With such positive labour relations, and the work style reflected in soaring sales and pre-tax profits, there must be a lesson for British management generally in the flexibility and responsibility the company gives it employees.

10

Probable developments

In Britain at present three trade unions are making a positive effort to introduce flexible working hours: the Association of Scientific Technical and Managerial Staffs (ASTMS), the Association of Professional, Executive, Clerical and Computer Staffs, and the National Association of Local Government Officers.

ASTMS is very keen on the flexible working hours system. One reason is that the workers it represents are those that are ideally suited to the system. Second, the system offers an ideal vehicle for increasing ASTMS membership, particularly in the City of London, as it obviously brings about a real liberation of the office worker from commuting congestion.

Clive Jenkins, the union's national secretary says, 'We have a responsibility to get our members more job satisfaction. The drive now is to organise the way London's workforce commutes.'

The ASTMS has really taken the initiative over flexible working in the last few months. In October 1972, the 450 staff at the head office of the London & Manchester Assurance Co. Ltd at Finsbury Square in London embarked on a flextime scheme. Its agreement was negotiated by the ASTMS.

The initiative came from the union which approached the

company after full discussions on the system. London & Manchester Assurance was chosen because it had a small number of staff (450) in one building, who had little contact with the public, except by phone. Its management agreed to set up a working party, which was supplied with a great deal of information by the union.

From this stemmed a rough outline of what was thought workable, and the union then met the board of London & Manchester Assurance for formal negotiations. They accepted the system and after four months' operations there are absolutely no alterations to be made to it. The only slight problem noted by the union's insurance secretary has been the variations in the attitude of department heads. One or two are not being as free as they should be.

The London & Manchester Assurance agreement is a decided advance in the progress of flexible working time in Britain. It allows a very generous amount of flexible time. This stretches from 08 00 to 10 00, 12 00 to 15 00 and 16 00 to 19 00. Core times are from 10 00 to 12 00, and 15 00 to 16 00, and there is a compulsory 30-minute lunch break. Employees have a personal record of hours worked (see Figure 10:1).

There are at least 15 major companies in the insurance field alone who have similar pilot schemes, or who are in a process of coming to an agreement with ASTMS. By 1974, the bulk of employees in insurance, some 250,000, are expected by the union to be on flextime. Manual workers in manufacturing industry seem to be suspicious of the system. However, it is becoming so popular with white-collar staff that the interest in, and desire for, it will surely rub off onto the shopfloor.

Local authorities, including Cheshire County Council, the Essex River Authority and the Civil Service are also at the forefront of interest and many trials are already in progress. Their situation in the centre of traffic-congested cities and their need for routine clerical processing make them ideally suited to investigating flexible working hours.

								Total	
Name J. SMITH						Personal number 4 6 2 4 6 2			
Week ending 22 April 1973									
FLEXIHOURS Employees personal record London and Manchester Assurance								DR	CR
	M	T	W	Th	F		Brought forward		2 00
In	0830	0820	0830	0830	0820	In		42 10	——
Out	1230	1240	1220	1230	1240	Out		——	62 40
In	1300	1320	1340	1300	1330	In		66 30	——
Out	1730	1730	1700	1600	1700	Out		——	85 00
DRs						DRs			——
CRs				1.00		Standard hours		35 00	1 00
Reason				Dentist		Total		143 40	150 40
Authorised by				JS.		Carried forward			7 00

Signature of employee _____ J Smith _____

Figure 10 :1   London & Manchester Assurance : employee's personal record of hours worked
Used as follows:
1   Add the daily times from left to right and enter totals in the appropriate debit or credit column.
2   Add the debit and credit columns.
3   Subtract the lower from the higher total to obtain the debit or credit balance to be carried forward.
Remember times are shown in hours and minutes.

The personnel manager of Lufthansa German Airlines believes that flexible working *can* be achieved in a continuous production technology, like the assembly lines in the automotive industry. However, management will have to make the process fit the system in such cases. In other words, vary the speed of the production, have a slower-moving belt during flexible periods, that speeds up during core time.

But once assembly-line working is abandoned, as many manufacturers are already planning once team working comes in, then flextime will really spread universally.

It is the white-collar workforce however that is most likely to gain immediate benefits from flexible working time—if only because it decreases commuting congestion. 'The blue-collar worker doesn't travel far from home to work', says Clive Jenkins, 'but the white-collar worker follows career advancement prospects into the big cities. Their transport arrangements, in London alone, are growing increasingly worse.'

'The reality of more and more people going to the same places, at the same time, is putting considerable strains on transport systems. Travelling is more expensive than it need be, and the present rigid working arrangements mean that eating arrangements are also difficult, because of the concentration of people having lunch breaks during the same hours in the middle of the day.

'This is where we came in. Why should people be packed into a dirty, noisy, stress-filled working environment? We as a union are now planning a specific metropolitan approach, based on flextime. We have some 50,000 people organised in insurance, two city banks have been captured and we have members in the Bank of England and Stock Exchange. We are generating a common influence through all these offices. I see flextime operating generally in the City of London within five years.'

This view on the growth of flexible working time over the decade is upheld by many with real experience of the system. Lindsay Pirie of Wiggins Teape, for example, says, 'If there are not 500,000 employees on flextime in the City of London alone in the next five years, I'll eat my hat.'

Pirie, an essentially practical man, believes firmly that managements should *implement* flexible working, rather than continuously debate it. 'There has been so much talk', he says, 'that people are making a mountain out of a molehill. But it's a very, very important molehill in terms of job satisfaction, productivity and sheer happiness.'

Appendix 1

Planning and implementation checklist

The following checklist identifies the main activities involved in the introduction of a flexible working system into a company. The checklist does not provide an individualised approach for special situations. What it does do is set up a framework and a series of starting points for essential planning and consultation procedures.

The checklist divides into three phases: preliminary analysis and choice of system; the trial period; implementation and follow-through.

Note that the recurrent feature in the operation is the element of consultation and feedback of opinion.

A   Analysis and system design

1   Identify sector of company suitable for trial of flexible working time. Criteria for suitability for trial include:

> Compact departments where there is adequate information about optimum staff level, average work content and work rate.

Department(s) reasonably representative of eventual area of application.

2   Conduct audit of personnel by department, to establish arrival and departure times per unit.

3   Ensure starting measures are available in units under study of labour turnover, absenteeism and work output.

4   Establish essential core times (when all employees must be present) within each unit.

5   Establish a common denominator core time between all units or within the group of units under study.

6   Establish arrival/departure/lunchtime time bands for each unit or group of units.

7   Decide the method of time recording/observation to be used; basic options:

Time clock with clocking in and out.
Time clock with voluntary entries in register.
Voluntary entries without clock.
Trust based system with no written records.

8   Note that, with mechanised systems, data processing can be used to provide information on hours worked, time spent out of the office, etc.

9   Establish limits for time credits and debits at week and month ends.

10   Establish rules for treatment of overtime or of authorised surplus credit.

11   Establish policy for treatment of business travel, sickness and other authorised absenteeism.

12   Check arrangements are adequate to cover safety manning and essential services, for example, keys, security, copying facilities, switchboard, etc.

B   Conduct of trial period

13   Confirm choice of trial department(s).

14   Discuss proposal in broad terms with union representatives and management heads affected by the trial, giving an account of:

> Advantages and disadvantages of flexible working time.
> Choice of systems available.
> Study requirements of trial period.
> Implications of subsequent extension of system.

15   Decide on outline of trial scheme, including timetable for:

> Pre-trial briefing.
> Trial run.
> Assessment period.
> Target date for extension of scheme if approved.

16   Establish budget for trial and permanent schemes, including elements for:

> Equipment costs, specially clocks, also print costs for time sheets.
> Compensation costs, specially for reduction of overtime.
> Office/overhead costs.
> Opportunity cost of management time.

17   Prepare memorandum for distribution to *all* staff setting out principles of flexible working systems and benefits to employees and the extent of the trial period, the departments affected by the trial and also assuring full consultation.
18   Conduct series of briefing and discussion meetings with employee groups, inviting and incorporating feedback.
19   At end of trial period, formulate results in terms of benefits to company (assuming results are positive) and complete cost/benefit analysis (see 16) by quantifying:

> Changes in the number of hours worked per employee.

Reduction in labour turnover and recruitment costs.
Reduction in overtime payments.
Increase in work output, plant utilisation or quality
levels.

20 Conduct ballot or questionnaire survey to establish:

Employee attitudes.
Basic acceptability (or otherwise) of system.
Opinions and requirements for modifications.

C *Implementation and follow-through*

21 In consultation with appropriate representatives, draw
together lessons of trial period, make modifications as necessary and prepare detailed set of rules or company manual.
22 Establish timetable for implementation.
23 Consult with and brief other sectors of company.
24 Circulate document setting out results of trial period and
give go-ahead for full-scale introduction of scheme.
25 Provide employees with ready-reckoner hours worked
calculator (not necessary but a nice touch).
26 Maintain close supervision of system and employee attitudes during period immediately after introduction.
27 Carry through periodic analysis of costs/benefits and
communicate results to employees.

Appendix 2

Fifty leading organisations using flexible working hours

Company	Location	Sector
Allen & Hanburys	Ware	Pharmaceuticals
Baird & Tatlock	Romford	Factory equipment
Bates Son & Braby	Southend	Solicitors
Bensons International Systems	Stroud	Office equipment
Birmingham Corporation	Birmingham	Local government
Bosch	Watford	Electronics
British & General Tubes	Slough	Engineering
British Oxygen	Edmonton	Chemicals
Cheshire County Council	Chester	Local government
Civil Service	Manchester	
Electromec	Northampton	Engineering
Ellis (Kensington)	Croydon	Contracting
Essex River Authority	Chelmsford	Local government
Findus	Cleethorpes	Frozen foods
Fisons	Loughborough	Pharmaceuticals
Glaxo Research	Greenford	Chemicals
Gordon & Gotch	London	Publishers
W. R. Grace	London	Chemicals
ICI	Harrogate	Chemicals
ITT	Hoddesdon	Engineering
A. & C. Jenner	Mitcham	Engineering
Lakeland Plastics	Windermere	Plastics

Legal & General	Kingswood	Insurance
Lloyds Life	London	Insurance
London Borough of Croydon	Croydon	Local government
London & Manchester	London	Insurance
Manufacturers Life	Stevenage	Insurance
Metal Box	London	Engineering
R. H. Nameplates	Winchester	Engineering
Norwich Union	Norwich	Insurance
Ofrex	London	Office equipment
Pearl	London	Insurance
Pfizer	Sandwich	Chemicals
Pilkington	St Helens	Glass manufacturers
Pitney Bowes	Harlow	Office equipment
Private Patients Plan	Tonbridge	Insurance
The Provincial	Kendal	Insurance
Riker Laboratories	Loughborough	Pharmaceuticals
Rothmans	London	Cigarette manufacturers
W. H. Smith	London	Stationery
E. R. Squibb	Birkenhead	Chemicals
Sun Life	London	Insurance
G. W. Thornton	Cheedle	Textiles
Tregear Thiemann & Bleach	London	Patent agents
Unilever	London	Household products
United Biscuits	London	Food manufacturers
Unwins	Chislehurst	Wine merchants
Wendt	London	Insurance
Wiggins Teape	London	Paper manufacturers
David Williams & Ketchum	London	Advertising

Index

Absence codes or symbols 35, 58–9
Absences 38, 57, 92
Absenteeism 16, 22–3, 45, 70, 73, 79–81 *passim*, 84–6 *passim*
Accounting period 23, 41, 45
Administrative costs 73
Administrative staff 35; *see also* White-collar workers
Allen and Hanburys Ltd 25, 39, 42, 69, 71
Arrival times 12, 13, 61–2, 65, 72
Assembly-line working 100; *see also* Production work
Association of Scientific, Technical and Managerial Staffs (ASTMS) 97–8
Attendance lists 30
Attitude surveys, *see* Employee attitudes
Authorisation 59, 60
Authoritarianism 68

Batch production 75
Bergerat Monnoyeur pilot scheme 22

Betriebsrat 26, 27, 29–31 *passim*
Boehringer Mannheim GmbH 39–41
Bolton, J. Harvey 15–16

Canteen workers 20, 24
Chauffeurs 20
Cheshire County Council 98
Civil Service 98
Clock cards 57–9 *passim*
Clocking 12, 31, 34, 38, 58, 65
abolition of 13, 20, 89, 91, 95
see also Time clocks
Code keys 39
Commerzbank AG, Düsseldorf 71
Commissionaires 20, 24, 53
Communications 15, 26, 93
Compensation, claim for 75
Computer 12, 13, 27, 59, 92
printout 38, 57
Confederation of British Industry 85
Conferences 58, 59
Contractual hours 12, 20, 46
Control point 13

Cooperation 22, 52, 55
Core time 9, 12, 15, 19–20, 22,
    23, 26, 28, 34, 45, 46, 75, 100
  two-part 20–1, 98
Cover 56, 57, 69–70
Credit time 12, 13, 16, 19–20,
    21, 23, 26, 29, 44, 47, 57–9
    passim, 71, 75–6
  accounting period of 41
  for additional leave 15, 45, 47,
    58, 68
  problems of 24, 74

Day release 60
Debit time 12, 13–14, 16, 19–20,
    21, 23, 26, 29, 41, 47, 57–8
Departure times 12, 13, 63, 65,
    72
Deputy 11
Diary sheet 44, 50, 51
Dishonesty 17, 51

Earnings 81
Efficiency, increase in 17, 34, 44,
    61, 72
Employee attitudes 14–16, 22–3,
    24, 28, 34, 41
  surveys 44, 49, 61, 69, 82
Equality, individual 21
Essex River Authority 98
'Expanded' day 73

Fatigue 85–6
Financial penalties 73
Flexible bands 20, 56, 72, 73, 75
Flexible periods 9, 22, 23, 26,
    28–9, 45, 100
Flexible working hours, flextime
  advantages and disadvantages
    of 15, 26, 45–6, 67–77
  cost of, *see* Time-recording
    systems
  definition of 12
  effects of 44, 61, Chapter 7
  employee attitudes to, *see* Em-
    ployee attitudes
  in France 22–3
  future of 100

  introduction of 23,   25–31,
    44–51
  limits to 57
  origins of Chapter 1
  pilot schemes 22, 56–61
  rules and guidelines of 44,
    46–7, 52, 57–61
  savings through 70–1
  and trade unions 97–8; *see
    also* Trade unions
  trial period of 44, 46, 51, 52
  in UK 23
  unjustified fears about 51
  varieties of Chapter 2, 26, 90,
    98
Flexible Working Hours (Bolton)
    15
'Flexi-days' 76
Flextime, *see* Flexible working
    hours
Flow production 75, 90–1
Forgetfulness 57, 61
Four Days, Forty Hours (Poor)
    80
Four-day week 76–7, Chapter 8
  in Australia 84
  in Britain 84–5
  in Canada 82–3
  cost problems of 84
  disadvantages of 85
  future developments of 86–7

General meeting 56
Gleitzeit 12, 24, 27–9 *passim*, 34,
    39, 43, 55, 70–1, 74, 90
'Golden handshake' 92
Group life assurance 91–2
Group working 69, 75

Haller, Willi 39, 41, 69
Heating 68, 73
Hengstler system 38–42, 43
Hillert, Herr 12
Holiday allocation 15
Holidays 23, 38, 45, 57–60
    passim, 76, 91, 95
Honour system 21, 23, 34; *see
    also* Trust
Human metabolism 69, 85–6

ICI 69
Identity cards 38
Initial memorandum 27–8
Insurance companies 97–8, 100
International Time Recording Co
    Ltd 34, 38

Jenkins, Clive 97, 100
Job satisfaction 68, 97, 101
Joint consultation 23
J. Walter Thompson GmbH 19,
    Chapter 3

Labour turnover 22, 79, 82, 84
L'Aménagement du Temps (de
    Chalendar) 22
Landau, Manfred 55, 61
Leisure 81
Lighting 68, 73
Liptons 86–7
London and Manchester Assur-
    ance Co 97–8
Losenhausen Maschinenbau 70,
    71
Lufthansa 34–5, 38, 70–1, 100
Lunch breaks 12, 13, 30, 35, 59,
    77
    compulsory 19, 21, 22, 58, 85,
      98
    flexible 28, 46, 56, 61
    statistics 64, 65

Mailing room staff 53
Malingering 17, 92
Management
    attitude of 90
    benefits to 16–17, 19, 24,
      70–3, 80
    disadvantages to 73–4
    and flextime rules 28–9
    initiative 83, 101
    and works council 26–7
Manning, *see* Cover
Manual (blue-collar) workers
    12–13, 20, 98, 100
Married women 45
Master clock 13
Medical Research Council report
    86

Medical visits 76
Messer Griesheim GmbH 73–4
Messerschmitt–Bölkow–Blohm
    system 11–17, 39, 55, 70, 71
Middle management 21–2, 95
Mitbestimmung 90
Morale 11, 22, 61, 68
Motor industry 70, 100

Opinion poll 14
Overtime 14, 23, 26, 28–9, 44,
    45, 57
    abolition of 89, 91
    non-payment of 12, 68, 75–6
    payment 14, 35, 47, 51, 52,
      58–9, 60, 70–1, 72
    reduction of 71, 75
Overtime credits 14

Pakcel Converters Ltd 33, 69
Parking 65
Payment on monthly basis 21
Pay slip 12
Peak periods 17, 23
Pilkington Brothers 20, Chapter
    6, 68, 70
Pirie, Lindsay 43–4, 51, 100–1
Poor, Riva 79–80
Powell, Sir Richard 85
Production costs 79
Production work 20, 21, 67, 69,
    100
Productivity 11, 16, 41, 65, 70,
    72, 79–81 *passim*, 101
Profit-sharing scheme 91
Project costing 13
Punched card/magnetic-tape
    systems 13
Punched cards 12, 13, 27, 38

'Quiet time' periods 31, 45

Ready-reckoner 13, 38
Recruitment 45, 71, 80
Redundancy 80
Responsibility, individual 20,
    23, 34, 61, 68, 74, 79, 95
Riddell, Malcolm 85

Roundhay Metal Finishers
    (Anodisers) Ltd   80–2, 86
Rush hours   15, 45, 68, 79, 81

Safety risks   57–8, 70
Sandoz AG   20–2
Schreiber, Chaim   90, 93, 95
Schreiber Wood Industries Ltd
    Chapter 9
Self-discipline   21–2
Share incentive scheme   89
Shift work   21, 35, 85–6
    rapid rotation in   86
Shopfloor committee   92
Sickness   16, 38, 47, 57–9 *passim*,
    70, 85–6, 92
Sidney Technical College School
    of Management   84
Single-status experiment   13
Spicer, Frank   80–1, 82, 86, 90
Staggered gliding system   35
Staggered work hours   11–12,
    24, 39, 41, 72
Staff consultative committee   55
Standard working day or period
    13, 24, 44, 46, 67, 77
Status differentials   20, 75
Steering committee   56, 58, 61,
    65, 68
Strike   95
Supervision   23, 67

Team work   57, 66, 67–8, 69, 100
Telephonists   20, 24, 31, 35, 69
Three-day system   86–7
Time clocks   12–14, 23, 27–8, 34,
    38, 39, 57
    abolition of   21
    see also Clocking
Time-keeping attitudes   24, 45
Time in lieu   59, 60, 75
Time lost   41, 70, 72–3, 92
Time meters   13

Time-recording equipment   23
Time-recording sheet or card
    21, 33–8, 74
Time-recording systems   26–7,
    29, Chapter 4, 57
    cost of   41–2, 73, 74
    in Germany   12
    manual   13, 33–4
    mechanical   34–42
    in UK   12–13, 34
Trades Union Congress   67, 71,
    74
Trade unions   25, 41, 67, 75, 82,
    83, 89, 97–8
    committee   92–3
Traffic congestion   11, 39, 55, 65,
    68, 98, 100
Transport   11, 47, 68, 100
Transport costs   81
Transport and General Workers
    Union   25
Travelling   15, 68
Treuenfels, Carl-Albrecht von
    29
Trust as basis of system   89, 95

Variable working time   11–12

Wage agreement   41
Watchmen   24
White collar workers   12–13, 19,
    23, 98, 100
    status problems of   20–2
Wiggins Teape   20, Chapter 5,
    69
Working conditions   14, 31, 68,
    69
Working week, shortening of   26
Work load   15, 24, 26
Works council, *see Betriebsrat*
Work off site   57
Work visits   59

DATE DUE